TENERIFE

LA PALMA - GOMERA - HIERRO

SEVENTH EDITION
1985

BY **TEODORO MARTINEZ**

TRANSLATED FROM THE SPANISH BY

SHARLEE MERNER DE ELSWORTH

PHOTOS BY

E. ALVAREZ

CATALAN IBARZ

DE LA ESPADA

EDICIONES GASTEIZ

DR. GUIGOU, 21, BAJOS

TEL. 27 75 85

SANTA CRUZ DE TENERIFE (SPAIN)

CONTENTS

PREFACE

A new guide to Tenerife has been published today. "Another one?" the native or the tourist will probably remark as he glances at it with a mixture of curiosity and scepticism. That is just what we do not want it to be, another addition to the long series of guides that have appeared so far. Not because of any literary pretensions which we might harbor, for little or nothing can we add to the serious studies of the island, but because the text is a historical and descriptive synthesis whose purpose is to enhance the photography.

Far from wishing to compete with other guides, we aspire after something higher. If in regard to the historical aspect, innovation is nearly impossible, it is not so in regard to the artistic presentation. The guide we are introducing today is intended to demonstrate the beauty of the incomparable scenery of Tenerife harmonize the grandiose with the delicate, the arid with the fertile, the lunar with the paradisiacal. These paradoxes of Tenerife's landscape can be found by the reader in the new GASTEIZ guide, in which black and white photography has been expressly eliminated in favor of the exclusive use of color so as to exhibit the subtle beauties of «this basket of flowers floating on the waves of the Atlantic». Thus we hope to surprise those natives who are still unaware of mysterious corners on their island and arouse the admiration of visitors when they realize how faithfully the photographs reproduce the scenes they have seen along the roads and paths of Tenerife.

It is a pleasant duty to express my deep gratitude to Mr. Rafael Delegado and Mr. Pedro Tarquis, who have so kindly helped to check the original, adding valuable observations culled from their knowledge and experience. These pages purport to be a faithful reflection of my personal experiences during my wanderings along the paths and roads of the island, but there is nobody better fitted than the reader to judge whether they conform to reality.

THE AUTHOR

THE «TAJINASTE» IN BLOOM IN LAS CAÑADAS ⟶

CREATION OF THE ARCHIPELAGO

It has been said that the Canary Islands are the result of a love affair between the sea and fire. Their complicated orography reveals their volcanic origin immediately, but when it comes to solving the problem of how they came into existence, the opinions of scientists are divided. We do not want to bore the reader with a list of names, so we shall limit ourselves to a brief and simplified explanation of the most popular theories.

Some think that the islands rose to the surface of the sea as a result of a slow, millenary process caused by successive eruptions of submarine craters. They are relatively young, not going back further that the Tertiary geological era. Others, however, favor the theory of the Lost Continent, which sank in historical times according to a legend that has left an imperishable mark on the mind of civilized man. In this case, the Canaries, Madeira and the Azores, as well as the Antilles in the Caribbean, would be the highest summits of the submerged continent. Such is the origin of the Atlantis tradition, the basis for which is to be found in Plato's dialogues, *Timaeus* and *Critias.* This theory launched by the Greek philosopher has fascinated poets and writers, among them our great *Cinto,* Mosén Jacinto Verdaguer, and has inspired the most beautiful notes in the musical genius of the incomparable Falla, who left the work unfinished. To demonstrate how vast has grown the bibliography around the Atlantis theme, suffice it to say that more than twenty thousand different titles have been written, some romantic, others, scientific in tone. As for being scientific, the theory was created because of the necessity for relating the flora and fauna of America, Europe and Africa as well as to explain the similarity of their coastal contours.

Some are of the opinion that the Antilles as well as the Canary Islands and Azores are the vertices of a huge triangular island which sank after the Tertiary as a consequence of contractions in the earth's crust. The surviving islands, dominated by the smoking plume of Teide, are explained as the mute witnesses of its existence. Possibly this great island could have been the bridge communicating America with Africa and Europe.

SAW-TOOTHED CRESTS; DEEP GASHES IN ENGLISMAN'S PEAK; IN THE BACKGROUND, THE SILHOUETTE OF TEIDE

A CYCLONE OF PETRIFIED LAVA, SEEN FROM THE SUMMIT OF TEIDE

TEIDE KEEPS THE SECRET OF ITS AGE →

VOLCANOES AND LAVA

Although the mystery has not yet been solved, the most accepted theory among geologists leans toward the volcanic origin of Tenerife and its archipelago. It must be admitted that the signs pointing to such a paternity are obvious. Both the proliferation of extinct craters and erosion by wind and torrential waters have given the island its present physiognomy.

Because of the recent appearance of the Canary Islands in history, we do not have sufficient facts to be able to reconstruct their geological history; we have barely known about them for six centuries. Nevertheless, we have recent historical references to various volcanic eruptions in Tenerife which have taken place from the time in the reign of Henry III when El Doliente erupted in 1393, witnessed by Biscayan sailors, to the epoch of Alphonse XIII and the ruption of Chinyero in the South of the islands, including a whole series of similar phenomena which have been duly recorded. Among them we many note the following eruptions:

— Orotava Valley in 1430.
— One noted in the diary of Columbus, which he witnessed as he sailed along the coast of Tenerife on the way to Gomera on his voyage of the discovery of America.
— Siete Fuentes (Seven Fountains) in 1604.
— Fasnia in 1605.
— Los Infantes in 1704.
— Los Roques in Güimar in 1705.
— Garachico in 1706.
— Chahorra in 1798.

But even more abundant as obvious evidence of its volcanic ancestry are the black and reddish lava flows which have run down the slopes from mountain top to sea, often forming overhangs and platforms, and known as *malpais* (bandlands or lava fields); the layers of volcanic rock called tuff; the great basaltic mountain spurs that form giant cliffs; rocks which have been violently distorted into savage shapes; and above all, proudly rising from the center of a huge ancient crater, the peak of Teide.

TENERIFE: FRUIT OF A LOVE AFFAIR BETWEEN FIRE AND WATER

TWO-FACED TENERIFE

Just like the god Janus, the island has two perfectly defined faces. It is the largest in the archipielago and bears a resemblance to a triangle; its three points are formed by Punta de Anaga in the Northeast, Punta de Teno in the Northwest and Punta de la Rasca in the South. If we can be permitted a rather crude comparison, we might say that the island is shaped like a huge ham floating in mid-ocean. Santa Cruz and La Laguna are to be found in the bone, and the ham is cut off at Punta de Anaga.

A long crest ridge runs across the island from northeast to southwest like the backbone of some monstrous dinosaur, and midway it opens into an amphitheater to form Las Cañadas Crater from which rises the peak of Teide. This cordillera divides the island into two diametrically opposed parts: the northern, green and humid; the southern, brown and arid except for green patches of vegetation which exist thanks to the titanic effort of man who has managed to tap the water from underground pockets found in the depths of the mountains and bring it by means of an elaborate network of tunnels and aqueducts to the thirsty lands of the South.

The cause of this difference in climates must be sought in the great wall of high mountains which acts as a barrier to the trade winds that deposit their moisture-laden clouds on the northern slopes. Here also we have the answer to why a ring of clouds usually surrounds the island and mitigates the summer heat. Such is the scene when viewed from the island of Grand Canary. Tenerife gives the impression of a sharp-prowed ship sailing along under a mantle of cotton-wool.

Naturally, where there is moisture, there is vegetation. Palms and banana trees, scatterings of red poinsettias and purple bougainvillea, orchards, fields of vegetables, vineyards, chestnut trees, beech and pine trees grow in succeedingly higher altitudes like a vast carpet which ends in fields of retama or Spanish broom at 2,000 meters (6,500 feet). And woven into this fabulous carpet, numerous white-stuccoed towns and villages form sparkling highlights.

In contrast, the other side of the island, even though falling less abruptly to the sea, is a harsher and more broken terrain. The water which is the hidden treasure of the island is less in evidence; there are fewer cultivated fields; the naked and terribly tormented mountains frequently reveal the scars of lava flows; green has turned to ochre; the place of shady woods is taken by scrub growth and cactus typical of sterile land. here

THE TRADE WINDS DROP THEIR MOISTURE ON THE NORTH FACE
OF THE ISLAND

man has had to battle with Nature, scratching a living from the infertile earth that left alone will support only cardoons, euphorbia, and other desert-type plants. His triumph is due to water.

← THE WAVE-BATTERED NORTH COAST

TENERIFE: THE MOST FORTUNATE OF THE FORTUNATE ISLES

AN EDEN

Tenerife is the most fortunate of the Fortunate Isles. Let our imagination carry us aloft in a flight such as interplanetary science now permits. Let us leave earth's gravity behind and soar upwards until we can look down on the group of islands that form the Canary Archipelago. They appear like a flock of doves who have gently alit on the sea after a tiring flight... In the center is Teide, usually white with snow, contemplating the group with the wide-open eye of his crater. How long have they been resting there? The secret of their origin is still unknown.

Today Tenerife is the talk of tourists all over Europe. Its name is uttered in all the tongues of the continent and of the whole world; it appears in every travel agency's brochures. what can be the reason for the island's attraction? Most of all it is the moderate climate that makes springtime last all year round. Rarely does the temperature descend below 15° C. (60° F.) or rise above 26° C. (80° F.) except when a hot wind blows from the Sahara.

What factors influence the gentleness of its clime? First of all the trade winds continually blow over the island, cooling it and at the same time facilitating navigation from North to South but hampering it in the opposite direction. Secondly, the sea-current of the archipelago maintains the coastal waters between 22° C. (71° F.) in summer and 18 °C. (65 °F.) in winter.

But there is another reason that brings people and often keeps them here, and that reason lies in the infinite variety of its landscape, which suddenly changes from a moonscape to a peaceful green valley, from massive mountains slashed by ravines and barrancos to the coastal belt of basaltic rock that forms cliffs overhanging the waves, or gentle slopes that fuse the gold and black of its sands with the azure of the sea. This is the key that explains Tenerife's success as an international tourist center.

TWILIGHT: THE SUN BIDDING A NOSTALGIC FAREWELL
TO TERRESTRIAL PARADISE

MAN

Poetry precedes prose and legend comes before history. All peoples have known the former before having the latter. What is known about the primitive people of Tenerife and the other islands? Very little, and even that is shrouded in the obscurity of legend.

The ancients knew it as the region of the Elysian Fields or the Garden of the Hesperides where the golden apples were guarded. Lost in the tenebrous Western Ocean from which sailors never returned, the islands were thought to be the Eden of the world, where the sun set and where Atlas with his conical form supported the celestial vault.

When the barbarians became masters of the fallen Roman Empire, the memory of the Isles of the Blest was lost. In the Early Middle Ages they reappeared again enveloped in the legendary penumbra of the Seven Cities, Saint Brendan (San Borondón) and Brazil. with the Renaissance they finally became a part of the Modern Age to serve as a bridge between the two worlds of Europe and America.

There have been many fanciful theories about the meaning of the name "Canaries". Is it derived from the singing canary bird or is the name of the bird taken from the name of the islands? Does it refer to the wild dogs (Latin *canis*) that certain visitors saw there? Perhaps it is easiest to derive the name from *Chernes,* which was that the aborigines called their islands.

In ancient times they were visited by Phoenicians and Carthaginians; the former gave them the name of «The Purple Islands» because of the reddish product they extracted from certain mollusks found in abundance along their coast. But we have no evidence that the Romans landed on the islands. King Juba of the African nation Mauritania sent an expedition there. A

←— A SYMPHONY OF COLORS IN EDEN

fleet of Biscayne ships explored them in 1393 and returned to Spain laden with slaves and local fruits. Those sailors witnessed one of the eruptions of Teide. At the close of the same century, many expeditions anchored off the beaches of the Canaries: Sevillians, Portuguese, Majorcans and even Genoese sent by the King of Portugal. On a navigation chart belonging to the Majorcan Angelino Dulcert, the Canary Islands are labelled «The Fortunate Isles».

THE SENTINELS OF TEIDE STAND GUARD

THE GUANCHES

The aborigines were cavemen called Guanches; the name seems to be derived from *Achineh,* which is what the natives called the island of Tenerife. If this is so, the word *guanche* would mean "man from Achineh" in the opinion of J. Alvarez Delgado.

Where did they come from? According to the hypothesis of the sunk continent of Atlantis, their land of origin would be Africa, for the short distance can be easily crossed. But this theory poses a problem that is not easy to solve. Historians and anthropologists have observed that the Guanches were not seafarers; they only fished from shore, mainly for shellfish, and never ventured out into the sea.

The skulls that have been discovered in the sepulchral caves where the Guanches buried their dead, show that they were basically a Cro-Magnon people with admixtures of Semitic and Berber. That there were various waves of immigrations seems to be indicated by the variety of cultures that can be observed from one island to another. The Guanche type seems to be best preserved in Tenerife. The first Europeans to come to the island before the conquest found a people of rudimentary neolithic culture with cutting tools made of polished stone, and living in caves. Their economy was mainly pastoral and they devoted themselves to raising goats, sheep and pigs, although they were also acquainted with agriculture, as can be seen from the *gofio,* toasted wheat or barley flour, which constituted the staple of their diet. They were ignorant of metals and urban living, and although they made very crude pottery, they did not have the potter's wheel, nor indeed any wheel.

The name "Tenerife" (in British English often written "Teneriffe") appears to mean «snowy mountain", an allusion to Teide, which the natives of La Palma saw dazzling white in wintertime. The Guanche language is not completely unknown to us, for we still find quite a few place names and some domestic tools with Guanche names. It is curious to note the large number of words that begin with the letter "T", for example, Tenerife, Teide, Tacoronte, Tanque, Taco, Tejina, Taoro, Taburiente, Tegueste, Tinguaro, Taganana, Teno, Tamaimo... Some scholars see a certain relationship with the Libyan language. Their social organization had the form of patriarchal tribes who obeyed chiefs or kings calles *menceys.*

UCANCA PLAINS AND TEIDE'S PEAK

NATURE'S CAPRICES

THE MUMMIES

In the museum of the Cabildo Insular (Island Council) of Santa Cruz de Tenerife, considered the best in the archipelago, we can study a series of aboriginal craniums, burial remains and reproductions of tombs. One of their customs that helps us to understand the guanches' religion is the embalming of their corpses. Ethnologists have seen a certain similarity with the Egyptian technique. For mummifying they used the sap of the dragon tree, the so-called "dragon's blood", with which they anointed the corpse several times and inserted it into the body through the mouth and nose, after having mixed it with aromatic herbs and sheep fat. After the anointment they left the corpse in the sun until it was completely dry. Then they wrapped it in a *tamarco,* a rough garment made of leather, similar to what was worn daily by both men and women. They sewed it extremely carefully, arranging the men with their arms stretched out and the women with their hands folded across their stomach. Then they buried them in inaccessible caves in the walls or on the brink of barrancos and closed the entrance with stones in order to prevent birds of prey from devouring them. All this tells us clearly that they worshipped the dead like the Egyptians and that they believed in the Beyond and in the afterlife of the soul.

The Guanches' religion was completely pantheistic; they worshipped the sun, moon, stars, the elements in general, and they offered sacrifices of milk, honey and sheep fat to strange rock formations. Their gods were

← THE DRAGON TREE, TOTEM OF THE GUANCHES

asexual and were never represented either pictorially or plastically; for this reason we find no traces of mythology in their religion. Like all primitive peoples, they believed in spirits and their influence on human life, especially the Spirit of Evil called Guayota. Above all these spirits or minor gods, they worshipped Abora, but they feared rather than loved him. This primitive religion is very far from the idea of the God of Love and the Redeemer of the Calvary.

RETAMA IN BLOOM BORDERING TEIDE'S PURPLE MANTLE

THE CONQUEST

Until the beginning of the fifteenth century, there were
no attempts at a formal occupation of the islands, but
merely sporadic contacts. The first expedition inter-
ested in taking the islands was organized by a Norman
knight, Jean de Béthencourt, an independent adven-
turer. He was partially successful and took possession
of several islands. Later, as difficulties arose, he was
compelled to ask the King of Castile, Henry III, for
protection, and received support in exchange for al-
legiance as his vassal. The Norman left as his succes-
sor a certain Menciot, who tyrannized the natives and
sold them as slaves, even those who has been baptized. The bishop, Don Menudo, raised his voice in pro-
test to the Castillian monarchs, who echoed the prela-
te's indignation at such injustice and authorized the
Spaniard Pedro Barba de Campos to buy the islands.
Barba in turn sold them to a Sevillian knight, Fernando
Pérez. The latter transferred them to his son-in-law
Herrera, who gave himself the pompous title of King of
the Canaries. Finally Herrera sold them to Ferdinand
and Isabella, all except for Gomera, and it was these
monarchs who decided upon the definitive conquest
of the whole archipelago.

CLIMBING TO THE SUMMIT —►

The first objective was the still independent Grand Canary, but Juan Rejón and Pedro Algaba's expedition failed utterly. Following them, Pedro de Vara gained a permanent foothold, while Fernández de Lugo carried out the conquest of La Palma and Tenerife. The Andalusian leader Lugo, of Galician origin, arrived before the present-day Santa Cruz de Tenerife with fifteen brigs on the morning of May 1, 1494. The place chosen to disembark was Añaza Beach. Quickly the news spread among the Guanche tribes who from their heights gazed horror-stricken at the "seahouses" which appeared on the horizon. Resistence was organized: an unequal fight of stone wea pons and sharpened lances with fire-hardened points, against harquebuses, swords and cuirasses. Lugo the *Adelantado* (military governor) advanced without difficulty up over Aguere, the La Laguna plain, passed through Los Rodeos Valley and had his first encounter with the foe in the barranco of Acentejo.

The *mencey* of Orotava, Bencomo, supported by his brother Tinguaro, had laid a trap for Fernández de Lugo, who fell into it and lost 800 soldiers in the battle. The Spanish leader, however, did not lose courage, but retired to Grand Canary to return November 2, 1495. Two battles were decisive; the first took place on San Roque Hill in La Laguna, where chief Tinguaro perished and his head was carried about on a stake through all the tribes, who were mourning the irreparable loss of their leader. The second, which determined the conquest, took place on Christmas Day, 1495, in Victoria de Acentejo. One by one the *menceys* Bencomo, Benaharo, Pelinor, Añaterve and others surrendered to the Spanish general. The definitive incorporation of Tenerife as part of Castile took place in the year 1496, and in the following year the *menceys* were presented to Ferdinand and Isabella in Almazán de Soria.

TEIDE FRAMED BY PINE TREES →

THE MONUMENT TO THE CIVIL WAR DEAD AND THE HEADQUARTERS
OF THE ISLAND COUNCIL

TRANSOCEANIC HARBOR

UNIQUE FLOWER CLOCK IN SANTA CRUZ'S PARK

EARLY SANTA CRUZ

Santa Cruz was the oldest port on the island, although not the most important. At first it consisted of no more than a landing with three steps where lighters tied up. Ar the end of the sixteenth century the port already boasted of a little mole and even shipyards to build ships for protection against the English, French and Dutch pirates which infested its coasts. The town started spreading out into streets: Blas Díaz, Candelaria, Cruz Verde, the earliest blocks of Calle del Sol and Barranquillo, the Church Square and El Cabo, where there were few buildings and which now marks the start of the highway from Santa Cruz up to La Laguna. For protection from the attacks of pirates, several forts were constructed, San Cristóbal in 1570, San Juan in 1648 and not long after, Paso Alto, which still survives converted into a museum; in it is preserved the cannon that shattered Admiral Nelson's arm in the Battle of July 25, 1797.

Two other ports on the island were close on the heels of Santa Cruz, Puerto de la Cruz and Garachico, from where the famous island wines were shipped to England and Holland. But these ports were slowly declining in favor of Santa Cruz, the only one authorized to trade with the Americas. The destruction of Garachico by the 1706 eruption left the way free for Santa Cruz to rise to its first zenith, in the eightenth century. Nowadays it is among the leading Spanish ports in incoming ship tonnage and in general cargo traffic. In 1983, 7,501 ships moored at its docks, having a total gross tonnage of 44,518,652 tons.

WHITE BUILDINGS IN SANTA CRUZ EXTENDING DOWN TO THE WATER'S EDGE

SANTA CRUZ DE TENERIFE AIR VIEW

BRIDGE BETWEEN TWO WORLDS

Even since Columbus landed in Grand Canary on 9th August, 1492, during his romantic adventure which was to culminate in the discovery of America, Tenerife has been the link between two continents. The bold Admiral sailed along its coasts with his heart set on Beatrice of Bobadilla, Lady of Gomera, where he stopped before heading into the unknown. While sailing round Tenerife, he witnessed one of Teide's eruptions, which he duly noted in his diary. That message of fire and smoke was a symbol; from then on, Spain was to count on this bastion not only to rest, take on provisions and refuel en route to America, but also as a merchandise clearing house and acclimatization garden for sugar cane, bananas, and other plants which were taken to the New World from Europe and Africa via this bridge. Tenerife was also the bridge for the potato and corn, which were introduced throughout Europe, the potato from Peru and corn from Mexico.

Santa Cruz de Tenerife is the last port that emigrants from Spain to South America sadly gaze upon and it is the first they greet when they are joyfully returning to their native land. Teide is the huge daytime lighthouse which they first catch sight of before they can see the outline of the island.

The Guanche mixed with the Spaniard, creating a strong and tall type of man and a remarkable beauty in the women. From that time on, there has been only one Spain, divided into peninsular and insular. The borders between the aboriginal and peninsular populations have disappeared completely as they have nowhere else in the world and the islander feels as Spanish as the man from the Peninsula. The islander is a descendant of both the Guanche aborigines and the Spanish conquistadors, or rather of their union. In the colored pages at the end of the guide there is a brief list of the names of some of Tenerife's native sons who have become famous in literature, arts and sciences, in the military and the Church. For Spain, the Canaries were not only a bridge to America, but a place of trial and test for its future colonial glory.

TENERIFE: A BASKET OF FLOWERS IN THE SEA

A FLOWER THAT BLOOMS IN THE AZURE SEA

As we have said before, Tenerife is a land of contrasts, a continuous-showing film of landscapes. In it go hand-in-hand the grandiose and the delicate; barren rock and peaceful green banana plantations; red or black lava fields and subtropical vegetation bordering barrancos or carpeting their depths; bare mountains with yawning craters and beech and pine forests covering vast stretches of their slopes; steep basaltic cliffs and long beaches that marry their golden sands to the blue of the sea. Rather than an island, we could say that Tenerife is a continent in miniature because of the contrasts and the variety of its landscape. But above all, its flowers are characteristic. We are not alluding just to those that grow in gardens or decorate the streets of the capital from the tops of the trees which border the sidewalks, such as the flamboyant with bright red flowers edged in gold, the jacaranda in a delicate lavender, or bougainvillea in a profusion of colors; we are referring also to those that grow wild by the roadside, on the steep walls of barrancos or peeping over village walls: poinsettias with fiery red over emerald green, immense fields of Spanish broom in Las Cañadas or *tajinastes* with a red and green plume waving high, giant campanulas, varieties of cactus beautified by the delicate simplicity of their blooms, such as *tabaiba,* cardoon, prickly pear, gorse, balo, and dye-plants like *cosco* and barrilla, not to mention the spring-blooming fruit trees. Tenerife is not only a basket of flowers floating in the crading waves of the ocean; it is a blossom that never dies.

POINSETTIA: RED AND EMERALD GREEN

A SOURCE OF WEALTH

Tenerife's income does not proceed exclusively from its great harbor and the oil refinery which is the largest in Spain, nor from the inestimable advantages of being a freeport, nor from the uninterrupted stream of tourists who visit its beaches and mountains all year round, but also from its agricultural products. The development of agriculture is the inevitable result of the titanic battle waged against a cruel Nature by men who have finally tamed her and obtained all sorts of crops. The perseverance of the native of Tenerife does not diminish when his emigratory impulses take him to other latitudes, especially to South America. The

THE BANANA PLANT PRODUCES ITS FIRST FRUIT IN 18 MONTHS

islander's labor there is greatly esteemed. Therefore, the river of banknotes that pours into Santa Cruz banks is the fruit of the tourist industry, agricultural labor performed by the Canario in Latin America and the export of island crops.

Tenerife has tried every kind of crop before the present ones. Successively through its six centuries of history it first established a flourishing international trade with archil, a lichen which produces a red dye, until chemical dyes killed the market. Then sugar cane enjoyed a brilliant period of prosperity. From here it went to America. The route followed by sugar cane from its native land to acclimatization in Tenerife seems to have been from India to Cyprus, Sicily, Madeira and Tenerife, where it took root and then crossed to Latin America. There, Tenerife was outproduced by the enormous cane crops of Cuba. After sugar cane, Tenerife's wines found wide markets in Europe with its renowned brands of *vidueño, listán, negramolle* and especially the malmsey or Canary sack that made Puerto de la Cruz and Garachico famous. After wine came barilla, a cactus plant that yields an alkali used in making soap, and then the cochineal insect, which was grown on the flat, fleshy leaves of the prickly pear and produced a renowned dye until superseded by the invasion of chemical dyes in the international market.

In sum, Tenerife has been a garden of acclimatization that has known a great variety of crops and still grows the products mentioned above on a large scale. In addition, it boasts a wide range of fruit trees adapted to its various climates, those typical of the north of Spain, like pear, peach, plum, strawberry, medlar, as well as the subtropical and tropical, like orange, mango, papaya, avocado, pineapple and so on, and the banana plant.

PLOWED FIELDS AND CROPS, FRUIT OF THE FARMER'S LABOR

THE DRAGON TREE

It might be a rather common-place topic, but Tenerife cannot be understood without either Teide or the dragon tree, one of the few Thousand-year-old survivors of a flora that must have at one time existed throughout the whole Mediterranean area. It is not a very exigent tree; it is not a bourgeois that digs its roots into the deep humus of virgin soil, but an equilibrist hanging from the most unlikely places, growing among rocks on cliffs. The dragon is a sacred, totemic tree that despite its forbidding aspect attracted the Guanche, who extracted from it a sap with curative and unguent properties. This sap was a commercial article in Antiquity and served as a cosmetic for Roman women; it was used as a specific to cure leprosy in the Middle Ages. Under the branches of the dragon tree, *menceys* administered justice. Its trunk looks like an anatomical drawing of a boxer's arms, and is prolonged by branches jointed like sausagelinks which end in balls from which sharp, swordlike leaves shoot forth to form a perfectly rounded tree-top. It is a sort of botanical monstrosity that seems through a thousand lonely years to have been longing for the companionship of a flora and fauna which disappeared in the Tertiary Era.

The best examples that still survive are in order of their beauty in Icod, the garden of the La laguna Seminary, and Los Realejos.

When European sailors landed in Tenerife, they were astonished to see the natives offer them dried figs in honey together with dragon tree blood. Even Dante refers to it when he says that the dragon tree sweats blood. The few trees that still remain are the last traces of a flora that must have covered vast areas in ancient times. Whatever their age might be, they closely guard the secret.

LAS TERESITAS BEACH

LIVELY GARCIA SANABRIA PARK

GENERALISSIMO AVENUE AND RESIDENTIAL ZONE

SANTA CRUZ DE TENERIFE

On the spot where the Spaniards landed in Tenerife, there grew up the beginnings of a town called by the Conquistador Santa Cruz de Añaza. He raised the cross of the conquest in the place today called El Cabo. Slowly the town grew until at the end of the sixteenth century it numbered a thousand inhabitants clustered together on the streets of Caleta, Blas Díaz, Candelaria and Cruz Verde.

The town was protected against pirate raids by several fortifications built at various dates. In 1657, it had to be defended against the English Admiral Blake, who had been tempted by the rich booty of galleons anchored in the port.

During the War of Succession, in 1706 to be exact, there was another attempt to take the island on the part of the English Admiral Gennings, who got nowhere when confronted with a heroic defense. Nelson also failed in 1797, losing the flags that today are on display in the Church of the Conception and an arm shattered by a cannon-ball from Fort San Pedro, according to tradition.

In 1822 Santa Cruz was named capital of the Canary islands and in 1859 was given the title of City. The division of the archipelago into two provinces took place much later, in 1927, after various failures in the previous century. Since then the province of Santa Cruz de Tenerife includes the islands of Tenerife, La Palma, Gomera and Hierro, and Las Palmas de Gran Canaria includes Fuerteventura, Lanzarote and Gran Canary.

The last historic date of great importance was 1936, when Generalísimo Francisco Franco, under the pretext of manoeuvres, met with garrison officers to plan the uprising of the 18th of July. This historic event is

MODERN EDIFICES IN THE CAPITAL AND HIGHWAY TO THE AIRPORT

commemorated by a monolith which can be seen in the forest of Las Raices on Mount Esperanza.

Santa Cruz is a bright and gay city with its white buildings spreading upwards from the sea into the surrounding rugged hills, protected from the winds of the North and East by the huge mass of the Anaga Mountains. It is a busy city with much commerce; yet it has not lost its colonial flavor despite urban expansion into beautiful avenues lined with jacarandas and flamboyants and with villas mantled in flowers and foliage. It presently has a population of some 200.000 inhabitants.

THE SPUR OF PUNTA ANAGA JUTS INTO THE OCEAN LIKE A SHIP'S POINTED PROW

SANTA CRUZ: PLACES OF HISTORICAL INTEREST

The proliferation of interesting ladmarks in Santa Cruz dates from the time of the greatests growth of the capital during the eighteenth century, once the reign of pirates was over. Since almost all its old build-

SANTA CRUZ CLOTHED IN SOFT BLUES AND GREENS

ings, religious and civil, date from that period, they are in the authentic baroque colonial style known as early Spanish colonial.

Worthy of mention among the civil buildings are Carta Palace on Candelaria Square and several mansions on Calle de la Marina, with typical balconies outstanding for their Canary pine woodwork. In the Plaza de España, facing the sea, the visitor is pleasantly surprised by the beautiful monument to the soldiers who fell in the Civil War, in the shape of a huge cross; in front of it stand stone guards, leaning on their swords. In adjacent Candelaria Square the first thing we see is a monument erected in honor of the patron saint of the island, the Virgin of Candelaria, carved in Carrara marble by the chisel of Pasquale Bocciardo, although often attributed to Canova.

Many large and small squares with an atmosphere of colonial-style architecture are worthy of special mention. They are quiet corners of the city that bring to mind monastery cloisters underneath the foliage of huge bay laurel trees. The most attractive is Weyler Square with the provincial military headquarters as a background.

Among the churches, the most outstanding is the Church of the Conception, oldest in the city, for it already existed in 1502. After it was burnt down in 1652, it was rebuilt in the seventeenth and eighteenth centuries at the height of the baroque period. The building mainly exemplifies this style, but its altars show the degenerate style called *churriguerismo.* Special mention is due the Weeping Virgin by the Canary religious sculptor Luján Pérez and also to the figure of the Conception which is set over the high altar, by Fernando Estévez of Tenerife. It is a Cathedral-church with five naves and a beautiful Baroque high altar made of jasper. In its interior are kept the Conquest Cross and a Gothic Virgin brought by the conquistador Fernández de Lugo, along with the flags seized from Nelson during the heroic resistance of the city in 1797.

Visitors are always impressed by the abundance of silverwork in many of the island churches. Silver covers its altarfronts, sacrariums and holy niches which, together with candelabrums made of the same metal, indicate that the acme of island prosperity was the eighteenth century.

The Church of San Francisco is also notable. It belonged to a Franciscan convent and displays two beautiful Baroque wood sculptures, one of San Pedro de Alcántara and another of Our Lord of Tribulations, although the latter statue is hidden under its clothing.

A FINE SILHOUETTE OF THE MONUMENT TO THE CIVIL WAR DEAD

WALKING THROUGH THE STREETS OF
SANTA CRUZ

There is a special charm in wandering through the streets of Candelaria Castillo and Bethencourt Alfonso windowshopping and browsing in the bazaars. This is a must for the visitor. Tenerife is not just landscapes and wonderful weather; it is also a great temptation to the shopper. Situated on the navigation routes to Latin America and Africa, its port, which every day extends more land into the sea to fill the needs of its new docks and warehouses, is continually visited by cruise ships full of tourists and transatlantic liners from all over the world. In Santa Cruz the tourist can find everything from whisky and tobacco to cameras and transistor radios, from silks to delicately carved ivory figurines from India —everything, and at lower prices than in the country of origin. The rare and the fancy, everything that can arouse a tourist's curiosity is to be found in shops crammed full of merchandise all displayed to entice the customer. It may seem odd that the prices of the articles are not shown in the shop windows, but that is because bargaining is the custom between buyer and seller, and the buyer usually prevails if she is a lady.

Santa Cruz takes pride in having a beautiful trapezoid - shaped park lying between Méndez Núñez Street and General Franco Avenue. It is worth even a short visit to admire the variety and beauty of its trees and plants, the big flower clock that greets visitors at the entrance, and the fountains with colored lights. It is called García Sanabria park in memory of one of the most famous mayors of the city.

Before going back to the ship, the visitor should take a look at the monument to General Franco, work of the sculptor Avalos, at the junction of Anaga Avenue and General Franco Avenue.

LA CANDELARIA SQUARE

SIGHTSEEING ROUTES

Choosing Santa Cruz as the starting point, we can tour the island following the three most interesting itineraries.

I. The Northen Route which ends at Punta de Teno and includes the following towns: La Laguna, Tacoronte, La Matanza. La Victoria, Santa Ursula, La Orotava, Puerto de la Cruz, Los Realejos, San Juan de la Rambla, Icod de los Vinos, Garachico, Los Silos and Buenavista. From different points along the route, secondary routes can be taken, some of which go through beautiful scenery and which we shall note in their place.

II. The Center Route following the central dorsal ridge of the island, as follows: La Laguna, La Esperanza, Las Cañadas, El Teide, Vilaflor, Granadilla.

III. The Southern Route follows the itinerary: Candelaria, Güimar, Fasnia, Arico, Poris de Abona, El Medano, Las Galletas, Los Cristianos, Arona, Playa de las Américas, Adeje, Playa de San Juan, Puerto de Santiago, Acantilado de los Gigantes.

From this third route secondary itineraries penetrate the interior of the island with its mysterious landscapes.

Because the space dedicated to text is subordinated to that occupied by the photographs, we cannot describe all the scenes to be visited but rather the ones we consider to be most important. We are also anxious to point out modern resorts and tourist developments, especially in the South, where sun-thirsty tourists flock, not to mention record-breaking Puerto de la Cruz.

← LAS CAÑADAS FLORA: «TAJINASTE» AND RETAMA

THE FERTILE PLAINS OF AGUERE

ROUTE I
LA LAGUNA

In spite of the fact that the conquistadors of Tenerife landed at Añaza and the first houses were erected there at the edge of the sea, the first town to obtain the category of city and become capital of the island was La Laguna. Its straight streets today retain the original old colonial atmosphere. It was founded in 1497 and from the first served as the official residence of the Adelantado, title given by Ferdinand and Isabella to the conquistador Alonzo Fernández de Lugo and later to the conquistadors of the New World. It is peaceful and clerical with mansions that bear escutcheons over their entrances, with hewn stone window and door frames under a habitually covered sky.

La Laguna came to resemble a court in miniature, complete with the four estates: ecclesiastical, noble, knightly and university. As for the ecclesiastical, La Laguna is the religious capital of the entire province, Tenerife, La Palma, Gomera and Hierro. its bishopric dates from 1818. It is a city of churches and convents and also is the seat of the university of the archipelago. It maintained its supremacy until the eighteenth century, when Santa Cruz superseded it as the capital. First the Adelantado, then the civil governor, then military headquarters were transferred to Santa Cruz by 1723. Political and administrative history are part of the city's history.

La Laguna is a university town par excellence with modern buildings that have replaced the old homes of the Augustine and Dominican priests who ran the schools. It is also the most artistic of all the cities of the island and we can add, of the whole Canary archipelago. It seems that time has stopped at its noble escutcheons, great church doors and straight, solitary streets frequently shadowed by a leaden sky that portends downpours and fog. In this city of episcopal and university descendancy, there is nothing more romantic than the slow drip, drip of the church and palace gargoyles or the measured tolling of its church bells.

At the entrance to the city from the main highways, after an ample vista of the wide plain of Aguere over which the city is spread, we are greeted by the monument to Padre José de Anchieta, Jesuit, apostle and colonizer of Brazil. This modern statue surmounts a pedestal brought there as gift from the South American nation to the native land of one of its most illustrious figures. The artist is the Brazilian Bruno Giggi.

THE ALMA MATER OF LA LAGUNA: THE UNIVERSITY

PANORAMA FROM ENGLISHMAN'S PEAK, DOMINATED BY TEIDE

LA LAGUNA: PLACES OF HISTORICAL INTEREST

We start with the cathedral, partly rebuilt at the beginning of this century, with its neoclassical façade; the interior is pseudo-Gothic. There are several wood sculptures by the Tenerife artist Estévez, among them a Magdalene, a Holy Christ and several Flemish panels in the retable of Los Remedios. In the church treasures a Virgin from the sixteenth century is noteworthy.

The most beautiful church is the sixteenth-century Church of the Conception, decorated by a Moorish-Canary panelled ceiling in polychromed wood from the sixteenth and seventeenth centuries. Its Baroque wood pulpit is perhaps the best work in the whole archipelago. There is also an interesting baptismal font of glazed ceramic from the fifteenth century and an unusual piece, a wooden tabernacle covered with copper. The processional Cross is made of silver repoussé as is the monument to Holy Thursday. The artist Luján Pérez has left his mark on a Weeping Virgin which the author considered his favorite work. We mention last a Purisima Virgin another carving, called "The Tears of San Pedro" by Estévez and the painting by Bocanegra from the seventeenth century representing the Immaculate Conception. This last has been declared a National Monument. Today the church is being restored because of the recent colapse of the coffered ceiling.

The Church of the Royal Hospital of Our Lady has an artistic high altar of polychromed wood. The ruined church of Saint Augustine, a dependency of the Agustine convent which is today a secondary school, preserves a cloister considered one of the best architectonic works in the city. We also should pay a visit to another church decorated with good modern frescoes and displaying a Magdalene by Estévez, the church of Santo Domingo, an old Dominican convent.

THE TORTURED IMAGE OF THE CHRIST OF LA LAGUNA →

If you want to satisfy your religious piety, we recommend a visit to the famous Christ of La Laguna, one of the most venerated saints in the Canaries; it belongs to the Convent of Saint Michael Victorious and in its church was buried the first *Adelantado,* Alonzo Fernández de Lugo. Today his remains are in the cathedral. The wooden statue is Gothic and was perhaps brought here in the sixteenth century at the beginning of the conquest. It is the second oldest church in the city.

We would never finish, if we were to examine minutely the other churches and convents of the city. Suffice it to mention Las Claras, the first convent built on the whole island, that has a beautiful panelled ceiling in its presbytery and other works of art. In the outskirts of town, the hermitage of San Benito is the object of one of the most popular pilgrimage festivals.

Among the civil buildings, note the Bishop's Palace and the mansion of the Marquis of Villanueva del Prado, called the Nava Palace. The university buildings are of modern construction.

THE NEOCLASSIC FAÇADE OF THE CATEDRAL

← PADRE ANCHIETA BIDS MELANCHOLY ADIOS TO LA LAGUNA

MOUNT MERCEDES

The excursion to Mount Mercedes is really worthwhile. Once across the broad, fertile lowland of La Laguna, we enter a dense forest watered by ubiquitous springs. Heather, ferns, beech and tall laurels envelop us in cool, dark shade until we reach the top, a peak called Cruz de Afur or Pico del Inglés (Englishman's Peak) after having passed through picturesque places like El Llano de los Viejos (Old Man's Flat), Llano de los Loros (Laurel Flat), Cruz del Carmen. The view that can be enjoyed from here is extraordinary. Precipitously - walled barrancos meander down to the blue sea. We can see both sides of the island dropping steeply from the central ridge that runs along the back of the island until it meets the impressive cone of Teide, lording it over the whole land.

TAGANANA IN ITS MOUNTAINOUS CIRQUE

CARPET OF VERDURE ON MOUNT MERCEDES

← A ROCK, MUTE, WITNESS OF PAST CONVULSIONS

NATURAL SWIMMING-POOLS FILLED BY OCEAN WAVES

An interesting side trip may be taken on the road which winds down from the Pico del Inglés to the junction with El Bailadero. There is a road to the left which leads to Taganana on one side of the island and a road to the right which leads to the fishing village of San Andrés on the other side. Nearby is Las Teresitas Beach, which is being developed by national tourist interests. From San Andrés the return to Santa Cruz is made by the coastal road, which is the ideal way to view the newly-constructed fishery basin as well as appreciate the gigantic dimensions of the harbor of Santa Cruz.

BAJAMAR AND PUNTA DEL HIDALGO

The sybarite of interesting and secluded spots will not be wasting his time if he takes the road from La Laguna that descends through Tejina, Bajamar with its complex of hotels, apartments and villas under development, and Punta del Hidalgo, and returns to the point of departure via Valle de Guerra. The road linking Bajamar with Punta del Hidalgo is a miracle of engineering cut into the rocky cliffs as if flying over the sea.

Color and light dominate Bajamar. The sun bathes everything constantly and is magically reflected in its large natural swimming-pools. Punta del Hidalgo has experienced the same tourist phenomenon, but there the old and typical refuse to desert the field. It is still a little while town retaining the atmosphere of a fishing village.

BAJAMAR ON ITS CLIFFTOP

PUNTA DEL HIDALGO IS A TONGUE OF LAND JUTTING INTO THE SEA

TACORONTE

Departing from La Laguna, the road to be followed crosses the green valley of Los Rodeos, site of the international airport. Then we reach Cruz Chica, from where we have a splendid panoramic view of Tejina and Valle de Guerra. Picturesque villages succeed one another. Just past the golf course we arrive at the junction that leads to Tacoronte.

We see fertile fields, vineyards, undulating hills that hide volcanic lava, while spots of villages scattered about... Nearby are the woods of Agua García, famous for its variety of flora.

Judging by the number of caves, the region must have been heavily populated by the Guanches; human remains indicating that the caves were destined for tombs have been found in quite a few of them. The main wealth of the town comes from agriculture, especially its famous wines. Nor has Tacoronte been left behind in the touristic field; witness the development of villas called Mesa del Mar.

From an artistic and religious point of view, Tacoronte is famous for the Christ of Tacoronte. It is a widely venerated image of an unusual form; it is not a common Christ Crucified on the Cross, but the Redeemer with his arms around it in a beautiful polychrome wood sculpture from the seventeenth century. The church preserves along with several other images one of the Virgen del Carmen by Luján Pérez.

Tacoronte's fine and delicate landscape is crowned by the silhouette of Teide in a way that is quite enchanting. The road continues on through more and more vineyards, banana plantations and even fields of sugar cane, all growing on a high plateau that drops over cliffs to the sea from a height that reaches 310 meters

FISHERMEN RETURNING FROM A DAY'S WORK →

(1,000 ft.) at Garañona. On the right we pass the village of El Sauzal, the villas of Los Angeles, the cave of Los Viejos, a curious Guanche dwelling, and the lookout point of Baranda, from where a breathtaking panorama of the north coast can be seen.

LA MATANZA DE ACENTEJO

One of the bloodiest pages of the conquest was written here, the slaughter of the Spaniards that were ambushed by the *mencey* Bencomo and his leader Tinguaro. The meeting of the two forces, Spaniards and Guanches, took place in the barranco of Acentejo. The name of the town commemorates this event (The Slaughter of Acentejo).

LA VICTORIA DE ACENTEJO

This is the other side of the coin. The town's name (Victory of Acentejo) commemorates the conquistadors' definitive triumph over the aborigines, that brought as a result the rapid submission of the *menceys* to the Crown of Castille. We pass green highlands and an abundance of banana plantations in the lowlands.

The conquistador Fernández de Lugo ordered built a hermitage to the Virgin of Victories in gratitude for his triumph over the natives. Close enough to project its shadow over the church, there still stands a majestic pine that marks the first belfry of Tenerife, because from its top the first bell was hung and in its shade the first mass was held.

Near the town a pottery shop is located, heir to the rudimentary Guanche technique. It is a pity that this simple craft is gradually disappearing. The road twists among vast banana plantations with palm trees rising out of them here and there, and the coast rises again above the sea. We pass through the town of Santa Ursula, whose rather ordinary church contains a good sculpture by Estévez, dedicated to Santa Rita, Suddenly, as if by magic, where the road forks, we stop and marvel before the grandiose vally of La Orotava.

TEIDE WHITE WITH WINTER SNOW

LA OROTAVA

In spite of having read all the publicity about it, a visitor is bound to be astonished when he contemplates this prodigious carpet of vegetation. It spreads out like an amphitheater, gently climbing until it mingles its green tones with the dark green of the pines that border the upper reaches of the valley and serve as a pedestal for the giant of the island, Teide, glittering white with snow in the winter, while below in the valley sun-kissed poinsettias are blooming. The valley extends some 62 km^2 (24 square miles) and in the middle, like a creche, lies the quaint town of Orotava. It is not surprising that the scientist Humboldt, on his way back from South America, fell to his knees before this scene, which recalled to him the tropics he had so recently visited, and he thanked God for the creation of this unique bit of land.

The Villa of Orotava is a typical example of a Tenerife town. Situated on the gentle slopes of a natural amphitheater, it is proud of the whiteness of its houses, a white interrupted by the dark tones of their Canary balconies and the many colors of the bougainvilleas which spurt from patios and flow over roofs as if they were flower fountains. It is an aristocratic town that shows its ancestry in escutcheons on mansions and in the marvellous Canary balconies where the valuable Canary pine wood called *tea* has been lavishly used. Quiet, monastery-like streets, neat gardens in public squares adorned with stone stairways, workshops of typical crafts such as those that produce the famous drawn-linen embroidery called *calado,* flower carpets on the cobblestoned streets to honor the Holy Sacraments in the procession of the Octave of Corpus Christi, water babbling through hidden irrigation troughs, flowers, gently filtered light, transparent air...

ARTISTIC CARPET MADE OF SANDS FROM TEIDE →

The parish church of the Conception with its fine architectonic lines contains, besides its silver and gold treasures, a marble and alabaster high altar in neoclassic style, product of the chisel of the Italian Gaggini, and good wood carvings by the famous Canary sculptors that have appeared so many times on the pages of this guide: a Weeping Virgin, a Saint John the Evangelist, and a Magdalene by Luján. The image of Christ Tied to the Column by Roldan in the church of San Juan and the two Virgins del Carmen and de Gloria by Luján are also worthy of note.

We have already mentioned the flower carpets of the Octave of Corpus Christi, customary throughout the whole archipelago. Let us point out that Orotava is the birthplace of this practice. One of the most beautiful carpets is the one that covers the Plaza del Ayuntamiento (Town Hall Square), with the difference that flower petals are replaced by fine gravel, in a rainbow of colors made from pulverized lava brought from Las Cañadas. Every year the furniture makers celebrate an exhibition of their hand-crafted products.

The road that twists up the valley slopes to Las Cañadas joins the one that comes along the central ridge in Portillo. Where the main road forks after Santa Ursula, one of the forks goes to Orotava while the other descends to Puerto de la Cruz; we shall follow the latter so as to stop at the Acclimatization Garden. It was built by Charles III of Spain for the purpose of acclimatizing plants from the New World for European climates. An illustrious patrician of Tenerife, the Marquis of Villanueva del Prado, maintained it out of his own pocket for some forty years, It is a splendid garden where we can find samples of species from all over the world and from every different clime. Then we continue on to Puerto de la Cruz.

CANARY-STYLE BALCONIES IN LA OROTAVA

FROM HIGH, YOU CAN SEE ALL OF PUERTO DE LA CRUZ AND →
MARTIANEZ LAKE

NATURAL SWIMMING-POOLS

MODERN VILLAS IN EL DURAZNO

RED POINSETTIA BLOOMING AGAINST GREEN BANANA PLANTATIONS ⟶

THE CLEVERLY-DESIGNED SWIMMING-POOLS OF MARTIANEZ

THE CITY OF TOURISTS SEEN FROM THE AIR

PUERTO DE LA CRUZ

Its name has an international flavor; it is famous beyond the coasts of Tenerife and the borders of Spain, moving in company with Torremolinos, Benidorm, Palma de Majorca and other world-renowned tourist resorts. For many years wine for Holland and England was shipped from this port, which depended on La Orotava. Today it is an independent municipality that blends its Old Town with luxurious, modern skyscraper hotels. Its mild weather, beautiful scenery and water sports attract thousands and thousands of foreign visitors who choose Puerto de la Cruz for their holidays or winter vacation. They can walk in the snow on the slopes of Teide and right afterwards take a dip in the sea or swimming-pool. It is the land where dreams come true for Scandinavians, Germans, English, French and Belgians who have invested their money in its modern villas and apartments and created a verita-

HIS MAJESTY THE CAMEL AWAITS RIDERS

THE OLD STRUGGLING AGAINST THE MODERN →

NEAT, ELEGANT STREETS

OLD CHURCH HIDDEN AMONG PALM TREES

ble Tower of Babel. It is important to mention the recent building of the Artificial Lake, on the coast of Martianez, the director of design is César Manrique; the extension was 33.000 sq. mts. taken from the sea, creating a beautiful place with a Lake of 15.000 sq. mts. and inside with 5 islands with night clubs, restaurant, bars, etc. all around are places to take the sun, sand and gardens. It is an old colonial-style seaport town built on a jagged lava field. Its main square shaded by the foliage of century-old bay laurel trees, its eighteenth-century church of Nuestra Señora de la Peña de Francia, the obligatory hermitage dedicated to San Telmo, the Franciscan convent and the religious wood sculptures of Luján and Estévez are the best evidence of its glorious past.

THE ART OF DRAWN-LINEN AND THE ARTISTS

← LIVELY CHARCO SQUARE

PROMENADE OF THE PALM TREES

BOOM IN CONSTRUCTION

INTENSE ACTIVITY, DAY AND NIGHT

THE OLD HARMONIZING WITH THE MODERN

LOS REALEJOS

We leave Puerto de la Cruz, one of the few places along the northern coast where the cliffs give way to gentle slopes that descend in an orderly manner out of the amphitheater of Orotava Valley to the sea. But immediately the abrupt coast again predominates and continues almost unbroken until past the Punta de Teno.

We have reached Los Realejos, a single municipality made up of two agglomerations: Realejo Alto (Upper) and Realejo Bajo (Lower). It was here where the *menceys* capitulated to the Conquistador and where the oldest temple of the island was built. The church in Realejo Alto dates from the end of the fifteenth century. In the parish house there are three paintings catalogued by Professor Hernández Perera as sixteenth-century Flemish from the Antwerp school. Tradition holds that one of the church bells was donated by Ferdinand and Isabella. One of the most valuable works is the baptismal font of jasper. In Realejo Bajo one of the three best examples in Tenerife of the dragon tree continues defying the centuries.

The road runs on through beautiful scenery, hugging the mountain through tropical vegetation along the Rabla del Castro or leaping over deep barrancos to bring us back to views of the sea, glimpsed over the high cliffs that tower above the azure water. we drive through San Juan de la Rambla, a town that seems caged between the sea and basaltic rock, and then we arrive at Icod.

A COUNTRY HOUSE HALF-HIDDEN IN FOLIAGE

ICOD DE LOS VINOS

The name of the town (Icod of the Wines) is indicative of its reputation for good vintages. Nowhere in the island is Teide nearer, nor can we see it better than from here. Icod is the capital of the lower part of the island and boasts a noble atmosphere in its aristocratic mansions and in the layout of its street in the form of a perfect cross. It is surrounded by leafy vegetation which carpets precipitous slopes and glens. Under the great trees of its plantations we see summer houses built for the enjoyment of the mild climate. Icod is not only the home of the wine that has made it so famous, but also an agricultural center, especially for bananas. There is nothing more charming than Cáceres Park, where giant bay laurels stand beside other graceful exotic plants.

Icod is proud of its parish church founded at the end of the fifteenth century and rebuilt in the sixteenth; the tower dates from the seventeenth. Besides its rich gold and silves treasures must be mentioned a San Diego de Alcalá, a polychrome wood sculpture by Pedro de Mena, and the sculptured retable from the seventeenth century.

Better known than its profitable vineyards and banana plantations is Icod's celebrated dragon tree, which is given such tender, loving care. It is the best one remaining on the island and the official town tree.

From here an excursion to the forest of Monte Castro is indicated. It is so dense and extensive that it is estimated to number about eight million trees. The town also has a nice little beach, San Marcos, sheltered in a cove below the cliffs, allowing swimmers to enjoy the water all year round.

HOW MANY GENERATIONS HAVE PASSED BY? →

From Icod a road takes off and climbs up to La Guancha, an extremely picturesque town with a scattering of cottages among its potato and grain fields in the middle of a wide valley that slopes gently towards the sea. In this ares we find a variety of vegetation, from the dry cardoon of arid lands to the alpine flora of the pine-forested mountain tops. This is made possible by the abundance of water here.

SAN MARCOS BEACH NESTLED UNDER CLIFFS

TEIDE SEEN FROM SAN MARCOS BEACH

EL TANQUE AND SANTIAGO DEL TEIDE

From Icod there is a road which leads to the South via El Tanque and Santiago del Teide. We follow its winding curves that overhang the land below and encounter a tremendous panorama of lands to the east and the bluish massif of Teno to the west. El Tanque is a good look-out point to enjoy the scene and, if the day is clear, we can discern the silhouette of La Palma undernealth its clouds. If we take the trouble to climb up through hawthorns and heather to the Atalaya (look-out-tower), we shall be vividly impressed by the sight of the giant lava flow that poured down on Garachico in the eighteenth century. The peak of Teide and Old Peak dominate the scene.

After passing through the grey and reddish mountains that ring it, we approach Santiago del Teide, a village hidden among poplar, cypress and almond trees. Here we have grain and vineyards, big farmhouses and old wine presses that signify the source of the town's income. This is where we can best appreciate the struggle man has waged to overcome rebellious Nature by the sweat of his brow in order to obtain bread and sustenance. The nationally-promoted tourist resort of Acantilado de los Gigantes is a dependency of Santiago del Teide and will be described in the section on the Southern Route.

ALMOND TREES IN BLOSSOM

GARACHICO

Four kilometers (2 1/2 miles) from Icod lies Garachico, half covered by lava from the 1706 eruption which destroyed a large part of the town, including the port and the sixteenth-century church. Founded in 1500, Garachico rivalled Puerto de la Cruz in the exportation of wines before both ports were eclipsed by Santa Cruz. In spite of the catastrophe of the eruption of Mount Bermeja de Trevejo, some noble mansions still remain, such as the seventeenth-century Baroque palace of the Marquis of Adeje. The church of Santa Ana is a good example of the fine art of woodwork and holds two important sculptures by Luján, Santa Ana and San Joaquín. The Castle of San Miguel, a fort built in 1575, still proudly stands defying the petrified lavas surrounding it.

LOS SILOS

Only 6 km. (less than 4 mi.) separate Los Silos from Garachico. Bananas grow very well in the alluvial soil found here and constitute the principal source of income. This is an oasis in the midst of the lava beds. In its mild weather, coffee and other tropical plants flourish. The parish church of Nuestra Señora de la Luz (Our Lady of Light) contains a beautiful seventeenth-century Baroque image of Christ Merciful by Juan de Mena of the Sevillian school. Along the coast are easily accessible beaches and coves while above us great pine forests shade the heights.

GARACHICO ON A PROMONTORY OF LAVA

SAN MIGUEL CASTLE

BUENAVISTA

The highway continues west until 5 km. (3 miles) from Los Silos where we reach Buenavista, a green and white scene of harmonious contrasts. This is the last town on the north side of the island. It lies tranquilly in the midst of a savagely wild landscape matching that of the other end of the island at Punta de Anaga. Beyond Buenavista lies the steepest and most mountainous part of the island, with great precipices overhanging the sea. Here we have the Teno massif; its gigantic wall challenges the ocean, the sound of whose waves dies half way up and never reaches the top.

From Buenavista a road goes along the coast to Teno Bajo (Lower Teno), situated on a windswept down. It is most impressive to see the lighthouse that stands there on a narrow-necked promontory.

The village boasts fine seventeenth and eighteenth-century manorial houses and its church dedicated to the Virgin of Los Remedios offers an artistic retable, polychromed Moorish-style coffered ceilings and a fine wood sculpture by Alonzo Cano representing Saint Francis. It was founded at the beginning of the sixteenth century.

A DRAGON TREE ON THE NORTH COAST →

ROUTE II
THE CENTRAL DORSAL RIDGE

This is the most interesting route from the point of view of scenery. We leave La Laguna and enter the forest of Mount Esperanza. From here most of the Canary pine has been obtained which was converted into baroque retables, balconies and regal staircases for manor houses. Canary pine gives *tea,* a noble wood that ages well and holds up in construction.

The highway winds through shady forest; the air is saturated with the heady scent of resin; sunlight filters through the branches and shines upon the carpet of pine-needles. We go past Las Raices (The Roots), where upon a stone monolith is engraved Franco's historic meeting date in 1936 that signalled the National Uprising.

The trees become thinner as we go up and up and reach El Draguillo at 1,500 m. (5,000 ft.) above sea-level. From here we have a tremendous view of both sides of the island, with the twin amphitheaters of Orotava Valley to the North and the Güimar Valley of the South. The scene could hardly be more Dantesque; sharp ridges and pointed crests, bottomless barrancos, the earth's cruist wrinkled like the skin of a pachyderm, dark green patches of pine woods, white villages highlighting a symphony of earth colors. But Lord Teide dominates it all, his cone broken off, gaping with a bitter grin at his failure to reach the sky. Everywhere on the slopes and on the crests we see volcanic cones, dead vestiges of prehistoric geological convulsions.

On our left we pass the road which goes to the meteorological observatory of Izaña at 2,360 m. (7,700

AIR VIEW OF TEIDE'S VOLCANO CRATER AT 3,716 METERS (12,191 Ft.)

DO THEY CLIMB TEIDE, TOO? →

ft.) above sea level. The highway carves its way through the dorsal ridge and reaches El Portillo de la Villa at the entrance to an enormous cirque surrounded by jagged peaks. Here the road from Orotava joins our highway after its ascent through the chestnut groves of Aguamansa.

A fine perfume dilates our nostrils; it comes from the pink and while flowers of the retama (a kind of broom). Its grayish green bushes grow in the black and brown lava. But in wintertime a while mantle of snow turns the scene into a monochrome. Sunlight falls pitilessly on obsidian and vitreous rocks that dazzle our eyes. We have arrived at Las Cañadas.

NATIONAL PARADOR IN LAS CAÑADAS

LAS CAÑADAS

Las Cañadas! Here we behold intense sunlight, air so transparent that the mountains become close enough to touch, a turquoise-blue sky, a moonscape with every kind of lava: pozzolana, basalt, obsidian, phonolite... and a whole rainbow of colors brought out by the sun: blue, red, yellow, white, black and most of all, ochre. we are facing a vast cirque of incredible dimensions, 12 kms. (7 1/2 mi.) in diameter and 75 kms. (46 mi.) in circumference. Rim and crater present a spectacle of sharp peaks, saw-toothed crests, grotesque rock formations twisted like giant reptiles in their death throes, and rising from the crater, the cone of Teide.

The series of level areas *(cañadas)* bear suggestive names such as Cañada de Diego Hernández, de la Angostura (Narrows), de la Grieta (Crack), del Montón de Trigo (Wheat Pile), and they are surrounded by a ring of mountains of various heights and extraordinary shapes: Montaña de Guajara, El sombrerito (Little Hat), El Cedro (Cedar), Montaña Rajada (Cleft Mountain)... Here and there are scattered eternally yawning craters.

From the height of our viewpoint at Los Roques, with Cañada Blanca behind us, we let ourselves be carried away in contemplation of the sharply defined scene before us after our eyes have become accustomed to the harsh light of the high altitude. The blinding whiteness of Ucanca Plain, sprinkeld with gray bushes, makes a sharp contrast to the nearly black horizon dividing the two zones. Within the frame of this geological picture which transports us into a lunar world, the pure, subtle air appears to be non-existent. We are enveloped in the impressive silence of high altitudes which leads us unawares into a deep meditation over the dawn of Creation.

In the middle of Las Cañadas the national *parador* hotel is located at 2,125 m. (nearly 7,000 ft.) above sea level.

Las Cañadas is a vulcanological museum in technicolor. In its stones the geologist can follow step-by-step the fearful history of periodic convulsions that have shaken the island out of its monotonous and humdrum daily existence.

VIEW OF LAS CAÑADAS AND TEIDE

TYPICAL COUNTRY RESTAURANT

UCANCA PLAINS

EL TEIDE

Its cone shoots skyward from the middle of the immense crater of Las Cañadas. Herodotus thought it was Atlas, rising so high that it disappeared into the clouds —the pillar of the sky. Various theories claim to explain its genesis. Some geologists maintain that it arose as a result of an unusually large explosion; others insist that it is all that remains of a catastrophic collapse of unheard of dimensions. According to the latter, the present cirque of Las Cañadas is what remains of the sinking of a higher mountain than Teide, consequence of a cataclysm that originated in the eastern half and later affected the western part.

No matter which theory is the correct explanation of its cosmogony, Teide is one of the most beautiful of monoliths, if such a paradoxical word can be used to speak of a volcanic conglomerate, or if you prefer, a free-standing mountain that rises 3,716 m. (12,191 ft.) above sea level; for the highest mountain is usually just a peak a little higher than the others that suround it in a range. Teide has the highest elevation in Spanish territory, 300 m. (1,000 ft.) more than Aneto in the Pyrenees or Mulhacén in the Sierra Nevada near Malaga.

On the southeast flank, like a baby at its mother's breast, Old Peak reminds us of one of the last eruptions, the penultimate to be exact, in 1798. The vast crater of Las Cañadas, which rings Teide like a crown, is a striking spectacle of a whole series of lesser and greater peaks which vary between 2,165 m. (7,000 ft.) and the 2,796 m. (9,000 ft.) of Guajara, third highest mountain on the island.

Teide tempts us at dawn or sunset to admire the great part of the Canary archipelago that can be seen from its top: Grand Canary, La Palma, Gomera and Hierro, which appear as if inlaid in a sheet of metal over which Teide projects its long shadow. The shadow gradually shortens as the sun rises over the horizon. Sublime, unique spectacle!

To make the ascent of Teide easier, a shelter has been built at 3,250 m. (10,700 ft.) at Alta Vista (High View). There climbers can rest the night before the final climb, usually made just before dawn, up to the very top. Thin fumaroles emanating from the summit crater and an acrid smell of sulphur are the last heartbeats of the colossus.

Nowadays a comfortable aerial cable car saves the tourist the exertion of a laborious climb. We should point out the two forms of life typical of Teide; animal is the Teide bird and vegetable is the Teide violet, whose soft color reflects that of the mountain at twilight.

We round out the excursion with a descent toward the South. At Boca de Tauce the road forks; to the right it goes to Chio and the Acantilado de los Gigantes (Giants' Cliff); to the left we continue on to Vilaflor.

TEIDE'S VOLCANO AND THE CABLE CAR TO CLIMB THE
HIGHEST PEAK

INTIMATE SECRETS WITH TEIDE AS WITNESS

VILAFLOR

If the descent takes places at dusk, the impression given by the great volcano is unforgettable; because of its purple robe it looks as if it were dressed like a nazarene in a Holy week procession. When we are heading down to Vilaflor, we suddenly catch sight of a giant griddle cake or an enormous cartwheel floating in the ocean; it is Gomera whose form and deeply-cut ravines justify the comparisons. Before we reach Vilaflor, an extraordinarily odd geological formation reminds us of Montserrat in Spain; eroded rocks suggest a monumental organ awaiting the fingers of an artist to interpret a Bach fugue on its keyboard. What a delicate landscape! Flat-pods and broom make a dense carpet at the feet of fabulous pine trees towering into the sky. Singing waters babble out of the mineral springs of Agua Agria (Bitter water) and Traste de Doña Beatrice; because of its digestive properties, this water is fit for any table. The woods become thicker as we go down, but in spite of indiscriminate lumbering, there still rise robust specimens that reach a height of 30 m. (100 ft.) and measure 8 m. (26 ft.) around the trunk. The road serpentines down through them, and suddenly around a bend appears a cluster of houses in a little hollow. This is Vilaflor, a village which subsists on agricultural and forest products, including many fruit trees. It makes a fine sanatorium for those who suffer from delicate lungs, considering its altitude of 1,400 m. (4,600 ft.). Its streets are steep and winding. A short visit to the church allows us to examine a good marble of St. Peter variously atributed to Siloe, the school of Michaelangelo, and others.

VILAFLOR: FOREST AND AGRICULTURE →

GRANADILLA

Down at 600 m. (2,000 ft.) Granadilla has virtually become the capital of the South. It is a picturesque town with winding streets where the old flirts with the modern without erasing the characteristics of either. Its wealth lies in the abundance of crops grown in its terraced fields: potatoes, legumes, cereal grains and vineyards. The pine forest of Vilaflor crowns it, while at its foot a desolate series of hills descends and peters out on the coast at the extensive beach of Medano. Nevertheless, the enterprising Canarians have succeeded in growing tomatoes on their barren lands, thanks to aqueducts that bring water out of the natural underground reservoirs found in the mountains. In the town, we are intoxicated by a perfume of orange blossom that pervades the air.

ROUTE III

THE SOUTH

The old, winding road that once separated Los Cristianos from the capital has been relegated to second plan by a splendid highway that brings the southern beaches to within an hour of Santa Cruz. This route goes over the bleak, dry side of the island; but by means of the miracle of water, black lava has been converted to magnificent banana, tomato and potato plantations. The basalt cliffs of the North are here replaced by gentle slopes that drop to a coastline characterized by small beaches and minuscule coves sheltered from the wind. Many tourist resorts are being developed, dotting the once desolate coast with lively, colorful oases.

The excursion to the South is made the highway that ends near Los Cristianos; but to see the towns and villages which are described in our intinerary, it is neccesary to take side roads that lead off the highway to the towns.

To the right as we leave Santa Cruz we pass the volcanic hills of Ofra and Taco. We do not stop at the modern villas and resorts of Radazul, Tabaiba or Las Caletillas, but continue to the village of Candeleria.

COLONIAL-STYLE TOWER OF THE BASILICA OF CANDELARIA

CANDELARIA

The town is a cluster of white houses that contrast with the black beach. Candelaria is the center of worship of the Virgin of Candelaria has been the goal of popular religious pilgrimages ever since it was founded in 1530 by Luis Cabeza de Vaca and maintained by Dominican priests.

The entire Güimar Valley is saturated with Marian piety. The story goes back to the end of the fourteenth century, when a statue of the Virgin was washed ashore by the waves of the Atlantic onto the beach of Chimisay. There it was found by a *mencey* of Güimar, who piously rescued it and carefully guarded it in his cave. For fifty years there is nothing but silence until a newly - baptized Guanche named Anton de Güimar transferred it to the Grotto of Achbinico, today called San Blas, where other Guanches were baptized. The second *Adelantado*, Don Pedro Fernández de Lugo, had a hermitage constructed for the Magdalene, where the statue was worshipped until 1530. Since that time the Dominican Fathers have been guardians of the foundation which supports the patron saint of Tenerife and of the Canary Islands. Unfortunately, the original image was washed out to sea by a landslide in 1826. The one worshipped today is a replica made by Estévez. The paradox is striking; the sea brought Our Lady and the sea took her away.

The sumptuous basilica was recently completed thanks to the Tenerife architect E. Marrero Regalado. Thousands of pilgrims flock to it from every corner of the island and during the holiday in honor of the patron saint on August 14, their number frequently surpasses 30,000.

THE VIRGIN OF CANDELARIA: QUEEN MOTHER OF TENERIFE →

Next on our way we meet the town of Arafo, which rises from among rivers of lava, surrounded by a belt of green vegetation and crowned with yawning, bare craters. Water running through is irrigation ditches gives exuberant life to vineyards, fruit trees, tomatoes and potatoes. This area must have been densely populated by Guanches, for we find numerous caves both sepulchral and habitable. Arafo boasts the famous Pino del Señor (The Pine of Our Lord) as well as several dragon trees.

THE LULLABY OF THE WAVES AT CANDELARIA

THE LEAST TALKATIVE ANIMAL

GÜIMAR

This is the twin or counterpart of Orotava Valley, but without the fabulous vegation carpeting the slopes of the latter. However, we cannot talk about an arid countryside. It is true that we see a great deal of black and reddish lava and a grey and white coast, but we also note extensive patches of verdure wherein lies the wealth of this region: bananas, potatoes, tomatoes, all kinds of fruits and vegetables. Güimar Valley is one more example of the stubborn struggle of the natives to overcome an ungenerous nature. The best view we can obtain is from the lookout point of the Mirador of Don Martín, a natural balcony overlooking an authentic Tenerife landscape. We feel that the spirit of the first *mencey* to submit to Ferdinand and Isabella. Añaterve, is still wandering through the barrancos and clefts of the valley.

Afterwards a quick trip to Puertito de Güimar (Little Port) and its urbanized area is compulsory.

FASNIA

Vegetation becomes thinner as we progress down the coast, giving way to varieties of cactus that hang on desperately to the inhospitable earth. We see barren coastlands and the lovely breast-shape of a young volcano, Mount Fasnia, crowned with a hermitage dedicated to Mary of the Sorrows.

Here not even the houses are white as they are everywhere else. They are constructed with blocks of beige tufa and blend in with the land around. A church and windmill in ruins make a romantic picture.

PANORAMIC LOOKOUT OVER GÜIMAR VALLEY

ARICO

Here we find a large municipality that spreads out to include 24 different hamlets. Once again, white clusters of buildings break the greyish-tan monotony of tufa and volcanic ash. We note shady little squares, quiet streets down which strolls his hunchbacked majesty the camel, draft animal of the South, equally accustomed to plow or cart. Here we can see best of all man's triumph over Nature, due again to the miracle of water. Arico is the potato-growing center of the island and also exports quantities of tomatoes.

Down below, the coast opens into a pretty bay protected by Punta de Abona (Abona Point) with its lighthouse and Punta del Carnero (Sheep Point). It shelters a little port called Poris de Abona, where new resorts have been built to take advantage of sun and sea.

The monotonous dry brown fields continue on to San Isidro. Here we can take a road on the right that goes to Granadilla or one on the left down to the beach at Medano, of fine white sand and the longest beach on the island.

We are passing through the place where we can find the international airport Queen Sofia-South of Tenerife, where the island can communicate with the other principal cities of Europe and America and the beach of Los Abrigos on our left, and enter the Costa del Silencio. Here, too, modern resorts and apartments have proliferated: Ten-Bel, Santa Ana, Santa Marta, Chayofita, etc. To one side we see the village of Las Galletas and in the background, the impressive panorama of Punta de la Rasca.

← WHO ARE THESE CHILDREN MAKING FACES AT?

THE LONGEST BEACH IN THE SOUTH

NEW RESORTS INVADE THE SOUTH

PANORAMA OF LOS CRISTIANOS BEACH, WHERE SHIPS LEAVE FOR GOMERA

LOS CRISTIANOS

The superhighway ends at Los Cristianos, the geographical center of this coast, where the sun never goes away on holidays. From its port there are maritime connections with Gomera. The clean, golden sands of the beach have radioactive properties that make rheumatic limbs and stiff joints limber once again. To prove it, there is the Swedish government sanatorium which receives Nordic patients in successive waves throughout the year in hopes of curing their painful maladies. Los Cristianos is rapidly becoming a resort for both islanders and foreigners with its modern tourist complexes.

After Los Cristianos a narrower road continues towards the beach of Las Américas, located within the municipal jurisdiction of Arona and Adeje. A fever of construction is rampant there; hotels, bungalows, apartments assure it of a splendid future within a few years. It is calculated that soon there will be 50,000 hotel rooms.

At Los Cristianos we can take the road to Arona, hidden among topless volcanic cones and bare rock formations, with a crest of pines in the heights above. In the range of mountains, two pointed peaks stand out, that the natives call Los Pechos de Arona (The Breasts of Arona). We must not neglect to mention the development of bungalows near there called Chayofa, the only one in the South not situated on the coast. Arona would be nothing more than that, were it not for the prodigy of water arriving over miles and miles of aqueducts to irrigate the extensive cultivations that in the future will increase even more.

COLOR CONTRASTS IN AN EXTRAVAGANZA OF SUNLIGHT

MODERN BUILDINGS INVADE THE BEACH

ADEJE

From Los Cristianos we go inland to this interesting town (See map) which evokes colonial memories with its aristocratic mansions. Time has respected such charming little corners as the environs of the parish of Santa Ursula. What a shame that functional concrete buildings are displacing the typical old architecture. The parish church contains a fine Moorish panelled ceiling and a collection of Gobelin tapestries, the only one on the island. They are in a lamentable state of deterioration, but fortunately now are undergoing restoration.

Another sight that must not be missed is the ruined castle Casa Fuerte, a feudal fortress and the former residence of the lords of Adeje. The economy is predomynately agricultural with a wide variety of crops.

The trip to the Barranco del Infierno (Hell's Canyon) is an impressive experience. It is exremely narrow with carpeted, vertical walls. Sunlight never reaches the bottom, 300 m. (1,000 ft.) deep. Above its ledges numerous Guanche funeral caves have been found. There is no doubt that the effort the aborigenes made to find inaccessible burial spots testifies to their cult of the dead. Adeje might be called the prehistoric capital of the island.

We leave Adeje and follow the coastal road. Along it we must point out the nationally-developed tourist resort called Callao Salvaje. We next come to the picturesque fishing port of San Juan, after which we advise a short visit inland to Guia de Isora.

WATER-FALL AT BARRANCO DEL INFIERNO →

GUIA DE ISORA

This town, at an altitude of 670 m. (2,200 ft.), seems to be taking a peaceful siesta in the sun on a lava bed of *malpais* below Old Peak. It is surrounded by almond and walnut trees, and towards the coast hundreds of terraces of banana trees and tomato fields. The whiteness and neatness of its houses draws our attention; here progress is the rule. As in other parts of the island, miraculous water from the gallery of Tágara has opened up the richness of the earth, giving so much water that the residents enjoy the luxury of tiny little reservoirs scattered around, sparkling in the sun.

Guia de Isora once boasted of a valuable retable in its parochial church. Even though it has disappeared, there is still a wood sculpture of Christ of the Sweet Death. In the lower part of town there is preserved a fine specimen of the mastic tree, and in the pine grove of Tárrega, one pair of pines have grown so large in girth that ten men cannot join hands around them.

We now return to our base of Playa de San Juan to continue along the coast to Puerto de Santiago, the end of our route. On the way, we pass Alcalá, well-known, along with Puerto de Santiago, for the sport of underwater fishing.

A ROSY FUTURE FOR LAS AMERICAS BEACH
THE FUTURE CENTER OF TOURISM ON THE ISLAND?

ACANTILADO DE LOS GIGANTES AND
PUERTO DE SANTIAGO

We are reaching the end of our tours, and perhaps the reader is weary of so much landscape description that necessitates repetition in spite of the great variety of scenery that Tenerife can legitimately boast. The last scene is left, but it is no doubt one of the grandest. Los Gigantes are gigantic cliff walls that reach a vertiginous height; at their base the waves smash against the basalt rocks and defeated, break into white spray. The visitor whose eye still retains the image of so many marvellous landscapes seen on his travels far and wide will shudder with excitement as he contemplates these immense walls. They rise through a symphony of colors like black giants from the azure sea. Lovers of underwater fishing find ample field to enjoy their favorite sport here at the base of this colossal rocky mass which plunges into dark blue depths. Beyond in the distance we can see. Punta del Teno, one of the three points of the triangular island.

With this last scene we have ended our tours over the roads and paths of Tenerife, the enchanting «basket of flowers» floating in the sea and which has afforded us so many suggestive impressions. The journey has been a film-showing of a procession of sharply contrasting scenes at every bend in the road, in which the grandiose harmonizes with the delicate, the tortured with the tranquil and the lunar with the paradisiacal.

THE BASALTIC MASS OF THE ACANTILADO DE LOS GIGANTES

FOLKLORE

Unconsciously men are influenced by the earth they tread, in such a way that their traditions become the living expression of the land around them. For this reason Tenerife, like every region of marked contrasts, has a rich and varied tradition folklore. It is neither European nor wholly of the New World, but rather unique. Popular traditions are manifested in songs, dances, costumes, sports and fiestas. Upon an aboriginal base, Time and History have created a folklore of typical characteristics with its own individual flavor but still belonging to the great Hispanic family of folklore.

One of the most characteristic notes of the world of folklore is the dance accompanied by song. In Tenerife, from what we can see and hear today, we can imagine what the Guanche dances were like. There is nothing more traditional and conservative than the legends and folklore of a region.

Judging from all the different kinds of Tenerife dances, those of the aborigines must have been executed with violent movements and acrobatic leaps. Among the most typical of the island dances are the *tanganillo;* the *saltonas,* a *jota* danced in a circle, which reminds us of the *fandango;* the malaguena, with its Andalusian flavor acclimatized to Tenerife and its choreography interpreting the contrast between the virile accents of a single male dancer and the gentler, suaver movements of girl dancers; the *santo domingo,* mainly a religious dance; and the *tajaraste* with its costume made of animal skins and feathers, the most typically Guanche dance, which spread beyond the islands, invaded European salons, and in Versailles was honored when the Sun King deigned to dance it.

Among the dance melodies, the *isa* with its Latin

American flavor and the *folia,* a variety of slow and aristocratic bolero, are both authentically Canary.

In this section on folklore, we cannot omit a description of the typical Tenerife folk costume, as colorful as

CANARY DANCES ACCOMPANIED BY GUITARS AND «TIMPLE»

the landscape. The *maga* (name of the Canary country-woman or peasant) wears a tiny straw hat that sits above her chignon and a brightly-colored headscarf that falls in folds down to her shoulders. Her blouse is of embroidered drawn-linen. Her full, striped skirt reaches her ankles. Black high-bulton boots and white stockings complete her costume.

The *mago* (farmer or peasant) wears a wide-brimmed, black felt hat, a while shirt, a black vest or one with black and blue stripes on a white background, short pants buttoned at the knee, and leather or wool leggings. To complement his costume he carries a long, thin staff used for driving oxen.

HOLIDAYS AND SPORTS

As in most Spanish towns, popular fiestas and *romerias* (pilgrimages) to a certain sanctuary, with folk-dances and celebrations, usually take place after harvesting, when everybody is contented with the abundance of the crops. It is curious to note certain customs of pagan Roman origin which were introduced to the island with conquest and colonization. One of them is the ship which sails on dry land; instead of cutting the waves, a boat in full sail is pulled by ox and cart through a sea of colorful regional costumes. This tradition is almost religiously observed in certain places, La Laguna, Las Mercedes and Tegueste, for example.

The most notable *romerias* are San Benito Abad in La Laguna in July, San isidro in La Orotaba, El Gran Poder de Dios and the Virgen del Carmen in Puerto de la Cruz, the Santísimo Cristo of La Laguna in September, and the Virgin of Candelaria, August 14, with its pastoral representation of the apparition of Mary.

GAY SCENES OF THE «ROMERIA» OF SAN ISIDRO →

Among the characteristic sports of the island and the whole archipelago, the most outstanding is *lucha canaria* (Canary wrestling), probably of Guanche origin. "This exercise in strength, entertainment and spectacle is no doubt of primitive origin, since it was especially noted by the Spanish conquistadors. It was also practiced by the Egyptians. Anyone who has even once seen *lucha canaria* will at once recognize it in the Beni Hassan reliefs, where more than 120 groups are depicted in various positions of the duel or two-man fight." (From J. Alvarez Delgado.)

In addition, most other sports are practiced on the Tenerife scene, especially nautical sports, snorkeling, scuba diving, underwater fishing, swimming and other aquatic sports. To these we can add tennis, claypigeon shooting, golf, etc. Nor can we omit cockfighting, though it is more of a spectacle than a sport.

HANDICRAFTS

Just a few words about Canary handicrafts. Outstanding are ceramics, woven straw hats and baskets, and the famous *calados.* This latter the first thing souvenir sellers thrust under the eyes of tourists when they step off the ship onto the pier at Santa Cruz. Is is the most typical of the island arts and crafts —the famous Canary linens, a fine drawn-linen work that requires extraordinary patience and is more often executed by individuals than workshops. It is produced all over the island, but mainly in Orotava. Puerto de la Cruz and Los Realejos. Without doubt it is the finest work of Tenerife and has brought the most fame.

«ROMERIA» OF SAN BENITO

CANARY HANDICRAFTS

LA PALMA

This is the greenest island of the Province of Santa Cruz de Tenerife, and with Hierro, the farthest west. Lava and tufa disappear under a layer of vegetation except in a few places covered by recent eruptions. Relative to its area of 726 km.[2] (280 square miles), it is the highest island in the world. The center is occupied by the biggest crater in the world, the Caldera de Taburiente, a national park, with a perimeter of 28 km. (18 miles) and a depth of 800 m. (2,600 ft.). It is an ancient, dead monogene volcano that offers extraordinary panoramic perspectives of torrents of water pouring down bare rocks; giant ferns and tall pines that scale the steep walls like ghosts; the sacred monolith Idafe, an altar where the Guanches worshipped their god Abora; and the whole grandiose abyss surrounded by the silhouettes of mountains whose inaccessible summits are frequently visited by snows. The highest peak is Los Muchachos at 2,423 m. (7,900 ft.), and there are enough others that surpass 2,000 m. (6,500 ft.) to cause in La Palma the odd phenomenon of being the highest island in the world relative to its tiny area.

The capital, Santa Cruz de la Palma, is a pretty town of 17,000 inhabitants, located in a natural amphitheater, with steep streets climbing up to the little crater of La Caldereta. It is situated on the eastern side of the island and enjoys an extremely agreeable climate like almost the whole island, with a mean temperature of 16°C. (66°F). Architectural landmarks are the church of El Salvador (The Saviour) and the Ayuntamiento (Town Hall), both from the sixteenth century. Along the seafront avenue big old houses with escutcheons are squeezed between modern edifices. There is a beautiful Canary-style national *parador* hotel with running balconies of *tea* (Canary pine).

THE LARGEST CRATER IN THE WORLD. CLOTHED IN GREEN

The town was sacked and burnt in 1533 by the French pirate Peg-Leg, who led 700 men to the attack. In 1585 La Palma residents obtained a complete victory over the squadron of the Englishman Sir Francis Drake after having sunk his flagship.

Like Tenerife and the other island of the archipelago, La Palma is of volcanic origin. Twice recently, in 1947 and 1972, there has been a resumption of volcanic activity but without notable damage and fortunately without loss of life.

It is worthwhile touring the whole island to see a new landscape at every turn of the road, but if you have little time, you must sacrifice all else to see first, Taburiente Crater from El Paso and second, the valley of Aridane in Los Llanos, which is to La Palma what the Orotava Valley is to Tenerife. It runs a close second to Orotava and is perhaps more varied. The view of it from El Time lookout is incomparable.

Near the villages of San Andrés and Los Sauces in the North of the island there is an extensive forest called Los Tilos, one of the largest and most beautiful in the Canaries. Fuencaliente, at the southernmost tip of the island, grows excellent wines and is especially famed for its *malvasía* (malmsey wine).

Another source of wealth for the island is the tobacco industry, producing several well-known brands of cigars.

In Mazo, near the airport, Guanche inscriptions have been found which, according to some archeologists, bear a certain relationship to those discovered in Libya. The name Guanche properly designates only the aborigines of Tenerife; however, it is also applied by extension to the primitive inhabitants of all the islands.

In a picturesque spot above Santa Cruz de la Palma there is to be seen the sanctuary of the Virgen de las Nieves (Virgin of the Snows), the patron saint of the island. In honor of the miraculous image, every five

THE GAY CAPITAL OF THE GREEN ISLAND

years a unique and unusually colorful celebration takes place. Many emigrants who have left La Palma for South America return in order to be present on this traditional occasion. Among the most typical spectacles of the fiesta are the Allegorical Cart, the Dance of the Dwarfs, the Dialogue Between the Castle and the Ship, and La Loa, a kind of miracle play presented when the procession enters the church of El Salvador.

THE HANDSOME COLONIAL-STYLE CHURCH OF EL SALVADOR

GOMERA

The view of La Gomera, as Gomera is commonly called, is captivating when seen from the heights of Tenerife. It seems as if you can reach out and touch its corrugated relief. It has been compared to a pancake floating in the waves, or to a cartwheel whose spokes are the deep barrancos which scar its suface. It is an island of rugged hills surrounded by a belt of basalt rock wich would prevent landing upon it, if it were not for the beaches and coves formed by the mouths of the barrancos at the coastline. Gomera is luxuriant and wooded, with a central massif called Garajonay, a perennial spring that supplies the entire island with water. Of its population of 25,000, 7,000, live in the capital, San Sebastián. Now this pleasant, pretty town boasts a magnificent tourist *parador* hotel in an eminently picturesque setting. Columbus stopped at La Gomera on his way to America for water and provisions and also to say farewall to his beloved Doña Beatrice of Bobadilla, mistress of the island. In the Church of the Assumption, still standing, he attended mass before setting out on his memorable enterprise across the Mare Tenebrosum. The Torre del Conde (Count's Tower), an ancient fortress now a national monument, commemorates this event.

SAN SEBASTIAN DE LA GOMERA

NATIONAL PARADOR IN GOMERA

One of the most remarkable things on the island, unfortunately on the way to disappearing altogether, is the Gomeran's whistling language. It had been transmitted from father to son until recently; children learned it along with their regular language. Until the use of the telephone supplanted it, it was the best means for communicating across the deep barrancos which separate villages from one another, and for transmitting rapid messages. It involves special techniques for articulating different tones of varying duration and volume, permitting it to be understood over great distances. A message is preceded by a call for attention from the sender and an answer from the receiver equivalent to "Ready". It is the only whisting language in the world.

Among the finest sights La Gomera, we must include the cedar woods, which vie with the best in the Canaries, and Vallehermoso, with its palms, bananas, fruit trees, savin, etc. We can also see a geological formation similar to the one found in Vilaflor in Tenerife —a giant natural organ. The biggest and best beach is in the banana-growing zone of Valle Gran Rey. Nowadays it has excellent maritime communications with Tenerife via the port of Los Cristianos.

LA ESTACA PORT IN HIERRO

HIERRO

It is the smallest and farthest west of all the Canary Islands. Its shape is a triangle of 278 km.^{2} (107 square miles). Of its 7,000 inhabitants, 5,000 live in the capital, Valverde. The center consists of highlands and its most elevated point is Mal paso at 1,501 m. (4,925 ft.). It is steep and mountainous with a coastline of cliffs falling sharply into the sea. Its mountains frequently open into craters while their slopes descend towards the sea covered with thick woods of pine, beech and savin. On the western side there is a large bay 14 km. (9 miles) long, protected by Punta de la Defensa and Punta del Salmor at either end.

The capital, Valverde, although small, ofters a pleasant picture among its orchards and gardens when seen from the sea. It has a handsome churchfortress. Among Hierro's products, wine is important, and at the South of the island fish are plentiful. The recently built airport is at 12 km. (7 miles) from the capital. Like La Palma, Hierro has its traditional Descent of the Kings' Virgin. The image is carried 35 km. (22 miles) across mountain and valley in fulfilment of a vow made after the end of a long drought. This fiesta is celebrated every four years in the month of May.

INFORMATION

We should like to express our thanks to the Delegation of Information and Tourism of Santa Cruz de Tenerife for its kindness in providing us with a great deal of the information found in these pages.

ILLUSTRIOUS PERSONAGES OF TENERIFE

The menceys BENCOMO, AÑATERVE.

Chief TINGUARO.

Padre JOSE DE ANCHIETA, Jesuit, apostle and colonizer of Brazil, born in La Laguna in 1534.

ANTONIO DE VIANA, poet, born in La Laguna in 1578.

PEDRO DE SAN JOSE, founder of the Bethlehemite Hospitalers, born in Vilaflor in 1626.

JUAN NUÑEZ DE LA PEÑA, royal chronicler, born in La Laguna in 1641.

GUILLEN DE CASTRO, sailor in the conquest of the Philippines, born in La Laguna in 1614.

VIERA Y CLAVIJO, historian of the Canaries, born in Realejo Alto in 1731.

AGUSTIN BETHENCOURT, scientist and philosopher, born in Puerto de la Cruz in 1758.

LEOPOLD O'DONNELL, general and statesman, born in Santa Cruz de Tenerife in 1809.

TEOBALDO POWER, composer, born in Santa Cruz in 1848.

IMPORTANT HISTORIC DATES

1393. Biscayan sailors explore Tenerife for the first time.

1492. Columbus sails around Tenerife on the way to Gomera.

1494. The Adelantado Alonso Fernández de Lugo begins the conquest.

1494. The Adelantado names Santa Cruz.

1495. Second attempt at conquest, successful.

1496. Incorporation of Tenerife into Castile.

1497. Founding of the city of La Laguna.

1657. Defense of Santa Cruz against the English Admiral Blake.

1706. Destruction of Garachico by an eruption of Teide.

1706. Failure of Admiral Gemmings to disembark.

1723. Military headquarters are moved from La Laguna to Santa Cruz.

1778. Santa Cruz is declared the only port on the island authorized to trade with the Indies.

1797. Victory over Admiral Nelson.

1803. Charles IV grants the city a coat of arms.

1818. Creation of the Bishopric of La Laguna.

1822. Santa Cruz de Tenerife is declared capital of the Canaries.

1859. Santa Cruz de Tenerife is named City.

1927. Division of the archipelago into two provinces.

1936. Meeting of Generalissimo Franco with his officers preceding the National Uprising of the 18th July.

TERRITORIAL AREA

ARCHIPELAGO, 7.543 Km^2 (2,913 sq. mi.).
TENERIFE, 2.053 Km^2 (793 sq. mi.).
LA PALMA, 728 Km^2 (281 sq. mi.).
GOMERA, 378 Km^2 (146 sq. mi.).
HIERRO, 278 Km^2 (107 sq. mi.).

INHABITANTS

TENERIFE, 505.000.
LA PALMA, 77.000.
GOMERA, 25.000.
HIERRO, 7.000.
SANTA CRUZ DE TENERIFE: 200.000.

MUSEUMS AND PLACES OF HISTORICAL INTEREST

SANTA CRUZ DE TENERIFE

FOR PASO ALTO. — Monument to the 1797 victory over Admiral Nelson. Displays the cannon «Tiger» which shattered Nelson's arm. Location: Avenida de Anaga.

CHURCH OF THE CONCEPTION. — Built during the XVI c. and rebuilt after it was burnt in the XVII c. It is the largest church, with five naves. In it are kept the valuable historical souvenirs of the Canarias, such as the Cross of the Conquest and the flags seized from Nelson after his frustrated attack on the city. Fine examples of baroque style. The Carta Chapel, of beautifully carved wood, and the handsome choirstalls, now in the presbytery, are also of artistic interest.

SAN FRANCISCO CHURCH. — Baroque façade from XVIII c. with twisted columns. The images of San Pedro de Alcántara from the same century and the Lord of Tribulations are remarkable.

MONUMENT TO THE FALLEN SOLDIERS. — Artistic monument with a graceful tower, lit at night. It is provided with a lift to the viewing platform at the top. Location: Plaza de España.

MONUMENT TO LA CANDELARIA. — It is in the square of the same name. It symbolizes the adoration of the Patron Saint of the archipelago by the Guanches, the primitive inhabitants. This monument was sculptured in Carrara marble in 1778 by the famous Italian artist Pascuale Bocciardo.

MONUMENT TO FRANCO. — At the intersection between Avenida Anaga and Rambla General Franco. Very modern features, built by popular subscription. Made by the famous sculptor Juan de Avalos.

ARCHEOLOGICAL MUSEUM. — Perfectly classified collections of skulls, tools and weapons, etc. can be seen, as well as facsimile reproductions of Guanche graves. It is in the Cabildo Insular (Insular Palace).

MUNICIPAL MUSEUM. — On José Murphy Street below the Plaza del Príncipe. It is also a painting and sculpture museum. Works of the best painters of Tenerife can be seen in it, as well as famous works by Ribera, Brueghel, Madrazo, Van Loo, etc.

CARTA PALACE. — It dates from the XVII c. with a hewn stone façade and a Canary patio. It is considered a National Monument of Artistic Interest. Location: Plaza de Candelaria.

INSULAR PALACE (Cabildo Insular). — Modern building of majestic design where magnificent paintings by José Aguilar can be admired.

MUNICIPAL PARK. — In its center stands the monument to Santiago García Sanabria, to whom most of the modern development of the city is due. There is an artistic flower clock at the entrance.

LA LAGUNA

CATHEDRAL.— Noted for balance and proportions of its columns, arches and vaults. The apse is beautiful; its presbytery is built on four marble steps with an unmistakable air of neo-Gothic. The choir, a legacy of Archbishop.Bencomo, is neoclassic. In the choir there is a lectern which holds a little crucifix by Domingo Estévez. The splendid organ was built in London in 1857. In the Chapel of Los Remedios there is a baroque altarpiece from the beginning of the XVIII c.

CHURCH OF THE CONCEPTION. — It is a tradition that the erection of this church was begun by the Conquistador. It was inaugurated in 1497 coincident with the beginning of the city's history. It has been declared a National Monument. As a whole, if offers a majestic perspective. The church treasury is rich in paintings, sculptures, gold and silver works by noted first-class artists.

SAN FRANCISCO CHURCH. — Where the Santísimo Cristo de La Laguna is worshipped. This image is lifesize, on a decorated panel of bornio wood from the early XV c., attributed to an anonymous artist of the Sevillan school. It was brought to Tenerife by the Adelantado Alonso Fernández de Lugo.

INSULAR PALACE. — Begun in 1542, Over its door, in plateresque style, in pink stone are carved the coast of arms of Charles V and the Coincullor Alvarez de Sotomayor.

PALACE OF THE COUNTS OF SALAZAR. —
Built in the XVII c. Grace and sumptuousness harmonize in the richly panelled ceiling of the interior. At present, the bishopric is located here.

PALACE OF VILLANUEVA DEL PRADO. —
Rebuilt about the middle of the XVII c., full of luxury and elegance, it was the meeting place of a well-known learned society from 1760 to 1770, whose director was the famous historian José Viena y Clavijo.

PUERTO DE LA CRUZ

CLIFFS OF MARTIANEZ. — Where the Guanches dwelled and from where the whole municipal area of Puerto de la Cruz can be seen.

SAN FELIPE CASTLE. — Old fort by the sea.

CHURCH OF NUESTRA SEÑORA DE LA PEÑA DE FRANCIA. — Built in 1603. Here the images of the Cristo del Gran Poder and the Virgen del Carmen, patron saints of the city, are venerated.

BOTANICAL GARDEN. — Acclimatization garden, founded by King Charles III in 1788. A veritable jungle in miniature, a complete collection of plants from all over the world.

SANTA CRUZ DE LA PALMA

TOWN HALL. — Built in 1563 in Italian Renaissance style. All the elements of its construction and exterior ornamentation are asymmetric, but so harmoniously blended that it is necessary to pay close attention to the detail in order to notice its asymmetry.

ROYAL CASTLE. — Example of a fortification built following the Vauban technique. It has been declared a National Monument. It is similar to the one built by Spain in Saint Augustine in Florida, also considered a National Monument by the United States.

NATURAL HISTORY MUSEUM. — It has wonderful zoological exhibits and aboriginal remains, as well as a splendid library.

CHURCH OF EL SALVADOR. — It is one of the most elegant and graceful religious structures of the whole archipelago. Its façade of hewn stone is Renaissance in style. Interior with Moorish panelled ceiling. The ceiling of the sacristy is Gothic, the only one of the island.

LIBRARIES, CLUBS AND SOCIETIES

SANTA CRUZ DE TENERIFE

PROVINCIAL HISTORICAL ARCHIVES. Castillo, 47.

MUNICIPAL LIBRARY. José Murphy.

SAILOR'S UNION. Av. Anaga.

CASINO OF TENERIFE. Plaza Candelaria, 11.

TWELFTH OF JANUARY FRIENDSHIP CLUB. Ruiz Padrón, 8.

FINE ARTS CIRCLE. Castillo, 47.

MERCANTILE CIRCLE. Plaza Candelaria, 6.

CONSERVATORY OF MUSIC. Teobaldo Power, 3

ROYAL AUTOMOBILE CLUB. Av. Anaga.

ROYAL NAUTICAL CLUB. Av. Anaga.

ROYAL SOCIETY OF PIGEON SHOOTING. General Fanjul, 17.

MILITARY CLUB OF PASO ALTO. Avenida Anaga.

LA LAGUNA

ATHENEUM. Plaza Catedral, 3.

UNIVERSITY LIBRARY. Avenida Universidad.

GOLF CLUB (Guamasa). Carretera del Norte.

RIDING CLUB. San Lázaro, km. 11.

ROYAL SOCIETY OF FRIENDS OF THE COUNTRY. San Agustín, San Agustín, 23.

SOCIETY OF PIGEON SHOOTING. Mesa Mota.

«PEACE» CHORAL SOCIETY. Sol y Ortega, 3.

PUERTO DE LA CRUZ

INSTITUTE OF HISPANIC STUDIES. Quintana.

SANTA CRUZ DE LA PALMA

TENNIS CLUB. La Caldereta.
ROYAL NAUTICAL CLUB. El Roque.

OFFICIAL CENTERS

SANTA CRUZ DE TENERIFE

CITY HALL. Viera y Clavijo, 34.
INSULAR CORPORATION. Avda. José Antonio.
MILITARY HEADQUARTERS. Plaza Weyler.
CIVIL GOVERMENT. Méndez Núñez, 5.
MILITARY GOVERNMENT. Avda. 25 de Julio, 1.
LABOR UNION HEADQUARTERS. Méndez Núñez, 76.
NAVAL COMMAND. Rambla General Franco.

LA LAGUNA

CITY HALL. Plaza Adelantado, 1.
LABOR UNION HEADQUARTERS. Ob. Rey Redondo, 11.

PUERTO DE LA CRUZ

CITY HALL. Iriarte, 2.
LABOR UNION HEADQUARTERS. Teobaldo Power, 21.

SANTA CRUZ DE LA PALMA

CITY HALL. Plaza de España, 1.
INSULAR CORPORATION. Avda. Blas Pérez González.
LABOR UNION HEADQUARTERS. Alvarez Abreu, 17

TOURIST OFFICES

SANTA CRUZ DE TENERIFE

PROVINCIAL DELEGATION. Marina, 59.
GENERAL ADMINISTRATION. Avda. José Antonio, 2.
INSULAR TOURIST COUNCIL. Avda. José Antonio.

PUERTO DE LA CRUZ

INFORMATION OFFICE. Plaza de la Iglesia.

EMERGENCY TELEPHONES

SANTA CRUZ DE TENERIFE

FIRE, 22 00 80.
FIRST AID, 24 15 02.
CIVIL GUARDS, 22 11 00.
POLICE, 091.

LA LAGUNA

FIRE, 25 10 80.
FIRST AID, 25 87 77.
CIVIL GUARDS, 25 94 16.
POLICE, 25 53 41.

PUERTO DE LA CRUZ

CIVIL GUARDS, 37 11 28.
POLICE, 38 12 24

SANTA CRUZ DE LA PALMA

FIRE, 41 11 50.
FIRST AID, 41 21 40.
CIVIL GUARDS, 41 11 84.
POLICE, 41 19 02.

OTHER USEFUL ADDRESSES

TENERIFE

POST OFFICE. Plaza de España.
TELEPHONE. Teobaldo Power, 6.
AUCONA-TRANSMEDITERRANEAN COMPANY. Marina, 3.
TOURING CLUB OF SPAIN. García Morato, 14.
ROAD CIVIL GUARDS. Finca Tío Pino.
NATIONAL SHOOTING CLUB. Polígono La Gallardina. La Laguna.
REINA SOFIA AIRPORT. Tel. 77 00 50
LOS RODEOS AIRPORT. Tel. 25 97 40.
TELEGRAMS BY PHONE. Tel. 22 20 00.

LA PALMA (Santa Cruz)

MAZO AIRPORT. Tel. 41 18 49.
AUCONA-TRANSMEDITERRANEAN COMPANY. General Mola, 2.
IBERIA AIRLINES. Miguel Sosvilla, 1.
TELEPHONE COMPANY. Pedro Poggio, 8.
TELEGRAPH OFFICE. Plazoleta del Muelle.

LA GOMERA (San Sebastián)

AUCONA-TRANSMEDITERRANEAN COMPANY. Gen. Franco, 41.
CITY HALL. Gen. Franco, 20.
TELEPHONE COMPANY. Av. José Antonio, 13.
CIVIL GUARDS. Calvario. Tel. 41.
NAUTICAL CLUB. Calle del Conde.

HIERRO .Valverde)

CITY HALL. Pérez Galdós, 3.
TELEPHONE COMPANY. Dr. Quintero, 4.
CIVIL GUARDS. Gen. R. Sánchez. Telephone 35.

FIESTAS

January 5. Three Kings Cavalcade. Santa Cruz de Tenerife.
February. Winter Carnival. Santa Cruz de Tenerife, Puerto de la Cruz and Santa Cruz de La Palma.
March and April. Easter Week. Santa Cruz de Tenerife and La Laguna.
May. Spring Fiestas. Santa Cruz de Tenerife
May. Descent of the Kings' Virgin. Every four years. Valverde (Hierro).
May 1-5. Commemoration of the founding of the city of Santa Cruz de Tenerife.
Corpus Christi. La Laguna.
Octave of Corpus. La Orotava.
Sunday following Octave of Corpus. Romería of San Isidro. La Orotava.
June 21-28. Every five years. the Fiesta of the Descent of the Virgin of the Snow. Santa Cruz de la Palma.
June 24. Fiesta of San Juan. Agulo (Gomera).
First Sunday of July. Fiesta and Romería of San Benito Abad. La Laguna.
July 16. Popular fiestas in honor of the Virgen del Carmen and procession in the harbor. Santa Cruz de Tenerife.
July 25. Fiesta of Santiago the Apostl. Commemoration of the defence of the city against Nelson's attack. Santa Cruz de Tenerife.
August, 5. Fiesta of the Virgin of the Snow. Santa Cruz de la Palma.
August 14-15. Fiesta of the Virgin of Candelaria, Patron Saint of the Canaries. Candelaria.
September 7-15. Santísimo Cristo. Fiest. La Laguna.
Sunday following September 17. Cristo de Calvario Fiesta. Icod de los Vinos.

CHURCHES

CATHOLIC

SANTA CRUZ DE TENERIFE

CRUZ DEL SEÑOR. Barrio del Perú. Tel. 22 19 33.
FATIMA. Plaza de la Arboleda. Tel. 27 74 20.

LA SALUD. Princesa Guacimara, 28. Tel. 22 13 05.

LA CONCEPCION. Plaza de la Iglesia. Tel. 24 23 84.

NUESTRA SEÑORA DEL CARMEN. Valleseco. Tel. 27 72 21.

NUESTRA SEÑORA DEL PILAR. Pilar. Tel. 28 36 48.

SAGRADO CORAZON. Horacio Nelson. Tel. 27 11 56.

SAN FERNANDO. Barrio de García Escámez. Tel. 24 45 62.

SAN GERARDO. Barrio Salud (Mil viviendas). Tel. 22 36 32.

SAN JOSE. Méndez Núñez. Tel. 27 36 62.

SAN PIO. Barrio de San Pío. Tel. 22 11 85.

SAN SEBASTIAN. P. Anchieta, 21. Tel. 21 74 38.

SANTA BARBARA. Barrio de Somosierra. Tel. 22 00 89.

SANTO DOMINGO. Barrio de la Victoria. Tel. 22 13 14.

LA LAGUNA

CATEDRAL. Plaza de la Catedral. Tel. 25 89 39.

CONVENTO SANTA CATALINA DE SENA. D. Palahi, 1. Tel. 25 85 30.

EL CRISTO. Plaza de San Francisco. Tel. 25 97 48.

LA CONCEPCION. Plaza de la Concepción. Tel. 25 91 30.

SAN JUAN. Pérez Cruz, 1 (Barrio Nuevo). Tef. 25 80 88.

SANTO DOMINGO. Plaza de Santo Domingo, 1. Tel. 25 92 75.

PUERTO DE LA CRUZ

LA PEÑITA. San Felipe. Tel. 37 22 02.

NUESTRA SEÑORA DE LA PEÑA DE FRANCIA. Quintana. Tel. 37 22 02.

SAN AMARO. Urbanización La Paz. Tel. 37 27 62.

SANTA CRUZ DE LA PALMA

EL PILAR. San Francisco. Tel. 41 19 04.

EL SALVADOR. Pérez Volcán. Tel. 41 15 88.

LA ENCARNACION. Plaza de la Encarnación. Tel. 41 21 72.

LAS NIEVES. Las Nieves. Tel. 41 11 37.

SAN FRANCISCO DE ASIS. San Francisco. Tel. 41 15 78.

PROTESTANT

SANTA CRUZ DE TENERIFE

ANGLICAN CHURCH. Plaza Los Patos, 7.

EVANGELICAL CHURCH. Avda. de Bélgica, 1. Tel. 22 33 39.

PUERTO DE LA CRUZ

ANGLICAN CHURCH. Parque del Taoro. Tel. 37 16 38.

CONSULATES

SANTA CRUZ DE TENERIFE

GERMANY. A. Anaga, 43, 1.º T. 28 48 12.

AUSTRIA. S. Francisco, 17. Tel. 24 37 99.

BELGIUM. San Francisco, 9. Tel. 24 11 93.

BOLIVIA. Lope de Vega, 6. T. 22 69 64.

BRAZIL. Castillo, 54. T. 28 65 12.

COLOMBIA. B. Alfonso, 25. T. 24 55 02.

CHILI. J.A. Delgado, 7. T. 22 78 98.

ECUADOR. C Peligro, 1. T. 24 32 87.

DENMARK. Avda. Anaga, 43. T. 27 57 57.

FINLAND. A. Anaga, 43. T. 27 57 57.

FRANCE. José María Villa, 1. Tel. 23 27 10.

GREAT BRITAIN. Suárez Guerra. Tel. 24 20 00.

ITALY. Pilar 25. Tel. 27 57 09.

LIBERIA. Betancour Alfonso, 25. Tel. 24 45 47.

MONACO. Pilar, 14. Tel. 28 25 50.

NORWAY. Tomás Zerolo, 14. T. 28 72 51.

HOLLAND. Marina, 3. Tel. 24 78 75.

PERU. Emilio Calzadilla, 1. 4.º Tel. 24 53 49.

PORTUGAL. Velázquez, 11. T. 22 69 73.

PANAMA. Puerta Canseco, 47. Tel. 28 86 08.
PARAGUAY. Rambla General Franco, 55.
Tel. 27 46 43.
SWEDEN. Avda. Anaga, 43. Tl. 27 74 50.
URUGUAY. 25 de Julio, 15. T. 27 69 65.
VENEZUELA. Pilar, 25. Tel. 27 33 16.
PAISES BAJOS. La Marina, 9. T. 24 35 75.
IRELAND. La Marina, 7. Tel. 24 70 46.

PUERTO DE LA CRUZ

AUSTRIA. Miramar. Ctra. Taoro. Tel.
37 11 67.
GREAT BRITAIN. Iriarte, 6. T. 37 25 00.

SANTA CRUZ DE LA PALMA

VENEZUELA. O'Daly, 31. T. 41 12 19.

BANKS

SANTA CRUZ DE TENERIFE

BANCO DE BILBAO, Marina, 3.
BANCO CENTRAL. San Francisco, 6 y 8.
BANCO DE ESPAÑA. Viera Clavijo, 37.
BANCO ESPAÑOL DE CREDITO. Plaza Candelaria, 8.
BANCO EXTERIOR DE ESPAÑA. Valentín Sanz, 17.
BANCO HISPANO AMERICANO. Valentín Sanz, 27.
BANCO IBERICO. Valentín Sanz, 25.
BANCO DE MADRID. San José, 17.
BANCO POPULAR ESPAÑOL. San José, núm. 16.
BANCO DE SANTANDER. San Francisco, 1.
BANCO DE VIZCAYA. Plaza de Candelaria, s/n.

PUERTO DE LA CRUZ

BANCO DE BILBAO, Iriarte, 17.
BANCO CENTRAL. Sargento Cáceres, 1.
BANCO EXTERIOR DE ESPAÑA. Plaza General Franco, 3.
BANCO HISPANO AMERICANO. San Juan, 9.

BANCO ESPAÑOL DE CREDITO. Avda. General Franco, s/n.
BANCO POPULAR ESPAÑOL. Nueves Ravelo, s/n.
BANCO DE VIZCAYA. Plaza Generalísimo, s/n.

REAL STATE AGENTS

SANTA CRUZ DE TENERIFE

CANARIAS. Numancia, 7. T. 27 58 00.
COBASA. Villalba Hervás, 5. T. 24 66 91.
DISCO VERDE. Pérez de Rozas, 27. Tel 27 81 53.
EUROCAN. Robayna, 8. Tel. 27 63 56.
FELIX MORALES RUIZ. Villalba Hervás núm. 1. Tel. 24 15 41.
FORTUNA. Villalba Hervás, 19. Tel 24 36 24.
HERMANOS MORALES RUIZ. Suárez Guerra, 63. Tel. 28 12 50.
INSULAR. Silencio, 1. Tel. 24 49 17.
JOVER. Rambla Pulido, 64. T. 27 70 01.
MANUEL GARCIA GONZALEZ. Pl. Weyler 5. Tel. 27 51 67.
MARTOS PAYA. San Clemente, 1. Tel 24 18 98.
MONTEMAR. Dieciocho de Julio, 17. Tel 22 68 34.
ORBE. Robayna, 8. Tel. 27 67 38.
PRINCIPE. Villalba Hervás, 21. Tel 24 42 97.
ROMAN MORALES RUIZ. Imeldo Serís, 77 Tel. 28 32 50.
SAN JOSE. San José, 2. Tel. 24 66 99.
SANTAELLA. Viera y Clavijo, 8. Tel 28 99 16.
TEIDE. Alvarez de Lugo, 45. T. 27 08 58.
TOMAS MORALES RUIZ. Sabino Berthelot 3. Tel. 27 58 50.
VALENZUELA. T. Power, 9. T. 24 26 45.

PUERTO DE LA CRUZ

CANARIAS. Avda. Venezuela, 7. Tel 37 11 86.

ANARIAS. Avda. Venezuela, 2. Tel.
38 00 86.
JROPA. Santo Domingo, 4. T. 37 22 39.
ORTUNA. Edificio Avenida. T. 37 29 19.
TERNACIONAL. Pl. Reyes Católicos. Tel.
37 13 55.
ELO. Avda. del Generalísimo. Tel.
37 15 99.
ANORAMICA. Avda. del Generalísimo, 10.
Tel. 37 16 19.
JERTO CRUZ. Esquivel, 7. T. 37 20 11.
ANTAELLA. Calvo Sotelo, 37. Tel.
37 28 52.

A LAGUNA

MOBILIARIA MARRERO. Obispo Rey Redondo, 18. Tel. 25 89 10.
ELO. Núñez de la Peña, 2. Tel.
25 80 22.

BOOK STORES

ANTA CRUZ DE TENERIFE

TLAS. Castillo, 70.
ILBAO, 25 de Julio, 4.
ATOLICA, San Francisco, 7.
ORREA. Sabino Berthelot, 1.
AVEGO. La Rosa, 44.
OYA. Pérez Galdós, 4.
ARA. 18 de Julio, s/n.
TERNACIONAL. Pilar, 29.
A PRENSA. Castillo, 68.
DUSA. 18 de Julio, 16.
COMAR. Cruz Verde, 7.
OBEL. Pilar, 13.
AYAL. General Mola, 79.
OLKA. Plaza Príncipe, s/n.
EXACHS. Robayna, 2.
XTO. Plaza Weyler, 4.
NIVERSAL. Castillo, 75.
PHEL. Avda. de Benezuela.
GU. Pl. Ireneo González, 9.

STATIONERY SHOPS

EL PRODUCTOR. San José, 20.
MADRID PARIS. Castillo, 59.
MERCANTIL. Pérez Galdós, 2.
NIVARIA. Imeldo Serís, 17.

PUERTO DE LA CRUZ

INTERNACIONAL. Avda. de Venezuela.
TENERIFE. Plaza del General Franco, 5.
TEIDE. Quintana, 2.

HOTELS

HOTELS - FIVE STARS

MENCEY. José Naveiras. Santa Cruz de Te-
nerife.
SAN FELIPE. Avda. Colón. Puerto de la Cruz.
SEMIRAMIS. Urbanización La Paz. Puerto
de la Cruz.
BOTANICO. Urbanización Botánica. Puerto
de la Cruz.
LORO PARQUE. Punta Brava. Puerto de la
Cruz.

HOTELS-FOUR STARS

TENERIFE PLAYA. Avda. Colón. Puerto de la
Cruz.
TIGAIGA. Parque Taoro. Puerto de la Cruz.
LAS VEGAS. Avda. Colón. Puerto de la Cruz.
LOS GIGANTES. Acantilado de los Gigan-
tes. Santiago del Teide.
PARQUE. M. Núñez, 32. Santa Cruz de Tene-
rife.
OROTAVA GARDEN. Aguilar y Quesada.
Puerto de la Cruz.
PARQUE SAN ANTONIO. Stra. Las Arenas.
Puerto de la Cruz.
EL TOPE. Calzada Martiañez. Puerto de la
Cruz.
MAGEC. Cupido, 17. Puerto de la Cruz.
LA PAZ. Urb. La Paz. Puerto de la Cruz.
PUERTO PLAYA. Polígono «San Felipe»
Puerto de la Cruz.

MELIA PUERTO DE LA CRUZ. Avenida Marqués Villanueva del Prado. Puerto de la Cruz.

MARTIANEZ. Avda. Generalísimo. Puerto de la Cruz.

CONCORDIA PLAYA. Avda. Generalísimo. Puerto de la Cruz.

NAUTILUS. Avda. Piscinas. Bajamar.

ATLANTIS. Playa Martianez. Puerto de la Cruz.

GRAN TINERFE. Playa de las Américas. Adeje.

VALLE MAR. Avda. Colón. Puerto de la Cruz.

BRUJA. Avda. Bélgica. Santa Cruz de Tenerife.

DANIA PARK. Cupido. Puerto de la Cruz.

ATALAYA. Parque Taoro. Puerto de la Cruz.

PUNTA DEL REY. Caletillas. Candelaria.

PARK TROYA. Playa de las Américas. Adeje.

LOS DOGOS. Urbanización Durazno. Puerto de la Cruz.

EUROPA. Playa de las Américas. Arona.

CALLAO SALVAJE. Callao Salvaje. Adeje.

RESIDENCE HOTELS - FOUR STARS

QUEBEY, A. Bethencourt, 28. Puerto de la Cruz.

HOTELS - THREE STARS

IKARUS. Urbanización La Paz. Puerto de la Cruz.

MONOPOL. Quintana, 17. Pierto de la Cruz.

MEDANO. Playa, s/n. El Médano.

CARIVER. San Telmo, 16. Puerto de la Cruz.

VALLE DE GÜIMAR. Carretera del Sur. Güimar.

DON JUAN. Pto. Viejo. Puerto de la Cruz.

MOREQUE. Avda. Marítima. Los Cristianos.

NEPTUNO. Ctra. Bajamar. Bajamar.

NOPAL. J. Antonio, 19. Puerto de la Cruz.

TINGUARO. Urbanización Moltalmar. Bajamar.

SAN TELMO. Sal Telmo, 18. Puerto de la Cruz.

DELFIN-LAGUNA. Bajamar. La Laguna.

MIRAMAR. Jardines Taoro. Puerto de la Cruz.

LOS PRINCIPES. Plaza Dr. V. Pérez. Puert de la Cruz.

INTERNACIONAL. Ctra. Arenas, 58. Puert de la Cruz.

TENERIFE TOUR. Las Caletillas. Candelaria

LOS VALOS. La Playa. El Médano.

REFORMA. Urbanización Tierra de Oro. L Realejos.

LAS AGUILAS. Las Arenas. Puerto de Cruz.

MAYANTIGO. Alvarez Abreu. Santa Cruz la Palma.

SAN BORONDON. Urbaniz. La Cherch Puerto de la Cruz.

MONNALISA. Pérez Zamora, 2. Puerto de Cruz.

RESIDENCE HOTELS
THREE STARS

BAJIO. Luis Lavaggi. Puerto de la Cruz.

TROVADOR. Puerto Viejo. Puerto de la Cru

CHIMISAY, A. Bethencourt, 14. Puerto de Cruz.

MARQUESOL. Esquivel, 3. Puerto de Cruz.

GUACIMARA. A. Bethencourt, 7. Puerto la Cruz.

TAGOR. Virtud. Puerto de la Cruz.

VICTORIA. Prolong. Puerto Viejo. Puerto la Cruz.

DIPLOMATICO. A. Nebrija. Santa Cruz Tenerife.

ONUBA. Blanco, 15. Puerto de la Cruz.

XIBANA PARK. Valois, 28. Puerto de la Cru

CASA DEL SOL. Finlandia. Puerto de la Cru

CONDESA. Quintana, 13. Puerto de la Cru

MARTE, Dr. Ingram, 22. Puerto de la Cruz

HARAL. José Antonio, 3. Puerto de la Cru

TROPICAL. Gral. Franco. 9. Puerto de Cruz.

COLON. Urbanización La Paz. Puerto de Cruz.

HOTELS - TWO STARS

ORO NEGRO. Avda. Colón. Puerto de Cruz.

BELGICA. Avda. Colón. Puerto de la Cruz

N MANOLITO. Los Guirres. Puerto de la
Cruz.

ARQUESA. Quintana, 11. Puerto de la
Cruz.

PRICHO. S. Fernando, c/. B. Puerto de la
Cruz.

AGA. Imeldo Sería. Santa Cruz de Tenerife.

N MIGUEL. José Antonio, 21. Santa Cruz
de la Palma.

RESIDENCE HOTELS
TWO STARS

AMPEREZ. J. Arroyo, 4. Puerto de la Cruz.

MAIDE. Gral. Franco, 108. Santa Cruz de
Tenerife.

N AMARO. Urbanización La Paz. Puerto
de la Cruz.

BURIENTE. Dr. Guigou, 19. Santa Cruz de
Tenerife.

LINOR. San José, 8. Santa Cruz de Tenerife.

O. C. Sotelo, 39. Puerto de la Cruz.

JOCHO. Ctra. Las Arenas. Puerto de la
Cruz.

ONSEVE. A. Bethencourt, 22. Puerto de la
Cruz.

ERTO AZUL. Lomo, 28. Puerto de la Cruz.

JUMA, P. Zamora, 51. Puerto de la Cruz.

HOTELS - ONE STAR

AGA. Iriarte, 7. Puerto de la Cruz.

N JOSE. Santa Rosa de Lima, 7. Santa
Cruz de Tenerife.

JAMAR. Rambla. Balamar.

S NUEVES, H. Alcázar. Guía de Isora.

LATTA. Urbanización Tabaiba. El Rosario.

RESIDENCE HOTELS - ONE STAR

EN. Prof. Plaza España. Los Llanos de
Aridane (La Palma).

MBI. Lomito. Puerto de la Cruz.

GUERE. Gral. Franco, 57. La Laguna.

SA ALTA. Calzada Martianez, 24. Puerto
de la Cruz.

ONICA. Pérez Zamora, 13. Puerto de la
Cruz.

ESQUILON. San Antonio, 62. Puerto de la
Cruz.

GARIGONZA. Camino del Pino. Granadilla.

ALFOMAR. La Peñita, 13. Puerto de la Cruz.

DON CANDIDO. Urbanización San Fernando. Puerto de la Cruz.

ROSA MARY. San Felipe, 16. Puerto de la
Cruz.

SILENE. Tomás Zerolo, 9. La Orotava.

LAS ROCAS. Puerto Viejo. 52, Puerto de la
Cruz.

CASA ROJA. M. Pérez Díaz, 43. Mazo (La
Palma).

RESIDENCE HOSTALS
THREE STARS

TANAUSU. Padre Anchieta, 4. Santa Cruz
de Tenerife.

UCANCA. Cruz Verde, 24. Santa Cruz de Tenerife.

PECEÑO. Pilar, 5, Santa Cruz de Tenerife.

MONTECARLO. Zamora, 23. Puerto de la
Cruz.

CAPITOL, S. Sebastián, 62. Santa Cruz de
Tenerife.

HOSTALS - TWO STARS

HOSTAL DEL DRAGO. Carretera General.
Icod.

RAMOS. Rambla Pulido, 93. Santa Cruz de
Tenerife.

REVERON. Gral. Franco, 9. Los Cristianos.

CAREL. El Médano. Granadilla.

BAMBI CAÑADAS. El Portiullo. La Orotava.

RESIDENCE HOSTALS
TWO STARS

MANROVI. San José, 6. Santa Cruz de Tenerife.

AROSA. Esquivel, 10. Puerto de la Cruz.

JORDAN. José Antonio, 4. Puerto de la Cruz.

PLAZA. Plaza Gral. Franco, 11. Puerto de la
Cruz.

TARAJAL. San Juan, 20. Puerto de la Cruz.

BALCON AL MAR. Avda. Cornisa. Bajamar.

PADRON. Gral. Mola, 106. Santa Cruz de Tenerife.

LAS MERCEDES. Iriarte, 29. Puerto de la Cruz.

PLATANERA. Blanco, 31. Puerto de la Cruz.

DUX. O'DALY. Santa Cruz de la Palma.

MIRAMAR. Avda. Anaga, 5. Santa Cruz de Tenerife.

LOLY. Sla, 2. Puerto de la Cruz.

RITA. Mequinez, 25. Puerto de la Cruz.

VIMA. Santo Domingo, 4. Puerto de la Cruz.

HOLM. Avda. Venezuela. Puerto de la Cruz.

AREA. Dr. Ingram, 15. Puerto de la Cruz.

LOS GERANIOS. Lomo, 16. Puerto de la Cruz.

MOVA. San Martín, 23. Santa Cruz de Tenerife.

BUNGE. Avda. Venezuela. Puerto de la Cruz.

VILLA DACIL. Playa San Marcos. Icod.

CANARIAS. A. Cabrera Pinto, 27. Santa Cruz de la Palma.

GARAJONAY, R. de Padrón, 17. San Sebastián (Gomera).

BOARDING HOUSE
TWO STARTS

VAZDEKIS. Montaña Tenisca. Los Llanos de Aridane (La Palma).

HOSTAL - ONE STAR

AGUSTIN Y ROSA. San Sebastián, 15. Icod.

MONTERREY. Carretera, Km. 1. El Paso (La Palma).

PLAZA. Plaza Iglesia, 14. Santa Cruz de Tenerife.

SORIA. Nava y Grimón, 18. La Laguna.

RAMOS. Heraclio Sánchez, 6. La Laguna.

ALEMANA. Piscina, 8. Bajamar.

LIBERIA. Cruz Verde, 1. Puerto de la Cruz.

VELAZQUEZ. Escudo, 10. Taco (La Laguna).

RESIDENCE HOSTALS
ONE STAR

NININA. Nieves Ravelo, 8. Puerto de la Cruz.

SOL. Zamora, 22. Puerto de la Cruz.

BAHIA. Plaza de la Luz. Santa Cruz de la Palma.

SANTA CRUZ. Castillo, 43. Santa Cruz de Tenerife.

FUENTES-ACHINECH. El Barco. Bajamar.

EL CARMEN. San Felipe, 7. Puerto de Cruz.

ASTORIA. E. Calzadilla, 7. Santa Cruz de Tenerife.

MORALES. Lic. Bueno, 7. Valverde (Hierro).

ANPER, B.J. Miranda, 4. Puerto de la Cruz.

MAR BELLA. Urbanización Los Bancales Los Realejos.

SANJURJO. Gral. Sanjurgo, 38. Santa Cruz de Tenerife.

ROSARIO. San Felipe, 4. Icod.

MARINA. Marina, 25. Santa Cruz de Tenerife.

CASAÑAS. San Francisco. Valverde (Hierro).

AMAYA. El Pazo. Vallehermoso (Gomera).

HESPERIDES, R. Padrón, 32. San Sebastián (Gomera).

RAMBLA. Gral. Franco, 68. Santa Cruz de Tenerife.

COLOMBINA. R. Padrón, 81. San Sebastián (Gomera).

RAMOS. Heraclio Sánchez, 6. La Laguna.

CANARIAS. Ruiz de Padrón, 5. San Sebastián de la Gomera.

CAPITAN. Plaza General Franco. Puerto de la Cruz.

SAN MIGUEL. San Miguel, 83. Santa Cruz de Tenerife.

APARTMENT HOTELS
FOUR STARS

EUROTE, - INTERPALACE Urbanización Paz. Puerto de la Cruz.

APARTMENT HOTELS
THREE STARS

BELAIR. Valois. Puerto de la Cruz.

GUAJARA. Avda. Generalísimo. Puerto de la Cruz.

MARTINA. Avda. Generalísimo. Puerto de Cruz.

LOS GERANIOS. Las Caletillas. Candelaria

GIRASOL. Dr. Ingram, s/n. Puerto de la Cruz

TEIDE MAR. Urb. La Paz. Puerto de la Cruz

PONDEROSA. Playa de las Américas. Adeje.
PRINCESA DACIL. Los Cristianos. Arona.

APARTMENT RESIDENCES
THREE STARS

COLON RAMBLA. Viera y Clavijo, 49. Santa Cruz de Tenerife.
EDEN ESPLANADE. San Fernando. Puerto de la Cruz.
PLAZA. Plaza Candelaria, 9. Santa Cruz de Tenerife.

APARTMENT HOTELS
TWO STARS

TEN-BEL. Costa del Silencio. Las Galletas.
BORINQUEN. Playa de las Américas. Adeje.

APARTMENT RESIDENCES
TWO STARS

LOGIS CHAMPAGNE. Mesa del Mar. Tacoronte.
FLORALVA. Calvo Sotelo, 17. Puerto de la Cruz.
MIMOSAS, E. Wolfson. Santa Cruz de Tenerife.
ROMANTICA. Urbanización Romántica. núm. 1. Los Realejos.
LAVAGGI. Avda. Generalísimo. Puerto de la Cruz.
PICAFLOR. Carretera Botánico, 6. Puerto de la Cruz.

APARTMENT RESIDENCES
ONE STAR

BANANAS. San Borondón, 4. Puerto de la Cruz.
AMARCA. Playa San Marcos. Icod.
CATRIN. Avda. Generalísimo. Puerto de la Cruz.

NATIONAL PARADOR HOTELS

The Ministry of Information and Tourism at present runs three national hotels called paradors in the province of Santa Cruz de Tenerife; Las Cañadas del Teide in Tenerife, Santa Cruz de la Palma on the island of La Palma, and San Sebastián de la Gomera on Gomera. All of them are three-star category with fine accomodation. On the island of Hierro, another one is going to be built in the Playas area.

GASTRONOMY

Canary cooking uses three essential ingredients in its typical dishes: fish in various forms, pork, and potatoes, called papas in the islands. Fish, mainly of the varieties known as cherne or sama, is generally eaten salted, salpreso, with a red sauce called mojo picón, and accompanied by papas arrugadas, which are unpeeled potatoes boiled in heavily salted water. Fish is also eaten fresh, especially the varieties known as vieja or sargo, grilled on the so-called salema and always accompanied by potatoes.

Potaje, a thick vegetable soup, is the basis of the diet of the popular classes. In general it is made with watercress, cabbage or zucchini squash, and potatoes. Puchero or cocido canario is a soup with the vegetables cooked whole in a tasty broth with a few chick peas and some sausage.

Pork is eaten adobado, cured, or salted and cooked with beans and green vegetables. when the broth is mixed with gofio, a flour of toasted grain, which is another basic food, then the dish is called escaldón.

Bananas and tomatoes, the main island crops, play an important role in Canary gastronomy, as well as gofio, which is sometimes eaten instead of bread with certain local dishes.

Among the sweets and pastries, rapaduras, made of honey and sugar, marquesotes, sugared sponge cakes, are from la Palma. Almendrados, almond cookies, come from Gomera and quesadillas, cheese cakes, from Hierro. A nougat made of honey and gofio or sugar and lemon, called turrón, is also made in the islands. Other delicious sweets are morcilla dulce, blood-pudding; tirijalas; bienmesabe; frangollo, a cornmeal pudding; sponge cakes; meat pies; and turrón made of molasses and gofio.

LOCAL WINES. Tenerife and the other islands produce excellent red and white table wines, and their malvasía (malmsey) and muscatel are universally famed.

Rum and honey-rum are native alcohols. As a magnificent complement to Canary cuisine there are excellent tabaccos, famed the world over for quality and variety, especially the cigars which are exported to many countries.

RESTAURANTS

SANTA CRUZ DE TENERIFE

ATLANTICO. Marina, 1.
BALNEARIO. Carretera de San Andrés.
BAVIERA. Rambla General Franco, 42.
CALLAO. Calleo de Lima, 2.
ESCUELA NAUTICA. Carretera de San Andrés.
CASA DEL MAR. Carretera de San Andrés.
CORYNTO. José Murphy, 1.
LA RIVIERA. Rbla. General Franco, 155.
HONG-KONG CHINA. Rambla General Franco, 141.
LA ESTANCIA. Méndez Núñez, 118.
PORTON DE ORO. Rmbla. General Franco, 39.
ROMA. Rambla General Franco, 48.
COLON RAMBLA. Rambla General Franco, 96.
EL AGUILA. Plaza del Alférez Provisional, s/n.

TIERRA MIA. Carretera de S. Andrés.
CHINA. Avda. de Anaga.
CORYNTO. Avda. de Anaga, 19.
DRAGON DE ORO. Avda. de Anaga, 2.
LAS MIMOSAS. Enrique Wolfson, 36.
EL GALLO ROJO. Rambla General Franco, 27.
GAMBRINUS. Primo de Rivera, 3.
LA MASIA. Castro, 13.
OLYMPO. Plaza Candelaria.

PUERTO DE LA CRUZ

ACUARIUM. Carretera del Botánico, 3.
ADELINA. Villanueva, 13.
BALCON DEL MAR. Punta Brava.
BAMBI. El Lomito.
BUFFET TOSCA. José Antonio, 1.
CASA ANA MARIA. Iriarte, 60.
CASA ANTONIO. Cruz Verde, 10.
CASA BLANCA. Cólogan, 16.
CASA CASIMIRO. Mequínez, 25.
COCK-PIL. Cólogan, 6.
CONDI. Avda. de Venezuela, 1.
CAPITAN. Plaza General Franco, 14.
CONTINENTAL. Avda. de Venezuela, 13.
COPENHAGUE, Dr. Ingram, 11.
CUBANITO. Dr. Ingram, 12.
CUPIDO. Cupido, 20.
CHOP-SUEY. Calvo Sotelo, 51.
DON QUIJOTE. Calvo Sotelo, 14.
EL COCHINO DE ORO. Zamora, 23
EL FLAMINGO. Dr. Ingram, 15.
EL GUANCHE. San Fernando, calle B. 3.
EL GUANCHO. Avda. de Venezuela.
EL MIRADOR, Plaza del Mercado.
EL PEÑON. Luis Lavaggi.
EL PESCADO. Transversa, Avda. Venezuela 3, B.
EL PICHON. San Telmo, 16.
EL PRESIDIO. Santo Domingo, 8.
EL TEMPLETE. Cupido, 27.
EL TIROL. Bajos Apartamentos Avenida.
GRANADA. San Felipe, 41.
FISH-FIETE. Valois, 52
HOLANDA. Prolongación Avda. Generalísimo.
HOSTERIA CASTILLO DE SAN FELIPE. El Peñón.

LA HERRERIA. Cólogan, 7.
LA HISTORIA. Carretera gral. La Vera.
LA ISLA. Valois, 49.
LA MARQUESINA. La Marina.
LA PACETA. Pérez Galdós, 7.
LA PAELLA. Avda. del Generalísimo.
LA RUEDA. Enrique Talg.
LAS CABEZAS. Canino, 23.
LOS PAPAGAYOS. Sitio Litre.
MADUQUE. Calvo Sotelo, 22.
MARINA. José Antonio, 2.
MESON LAS GALLETAS. Calvo Sotelo, 12.
MI VACA Y YO. Cruz Verde, 8.
OASUS CUEVA. Avda. de Venezuela.
OTTO (BEIM-DICKEN). Avda. de Venezuela, 3.
PATIO CANARIO. Cruz Verde.
PUERTO ESCONDIDO. Las Lonjas.
RANCHO GRANDE. San Telmo, 8.
SAN BORONDON. Los Guirres.
SAN MIGUEL. Calle del Pozo.
SANCHO PANZA. Iriarte, 36.
SVEND'S DROP-INN. Iriarte, 28.
TOLEDO. Iriarte, 29.
TRES CORONAS. Iriarte, 7.
UNION. Avda. de Venezuela, 6.
VICTORIA. San Borondón.
VIEJO HOLANDES. San Telmo, 12.
VILLAVISTA. Urbanización La Paz.

TRANSPORTATION

AIR

Regular service with the Peninsula: Madrid, Barcelona, Seville, Valencia and Malaga.
Interinsular: To Las Palmas, frequent daily flights; Arrecife de Lanzarote, Fuerteventura, Santa Cruz de la Palma, several daily flights; Hierro, daily flight.
International: Germany, France, England, Sweden, etc.

SEA

Daily service with Las Palmas, and via Las Palmas, with Arrecife (Lanzarote) and Puerto Rosario (Fuerteventura). with La Palma, Tuesday, Thursday and Saturday. With La Gomera, Monday and Tuesday from Santa Cruz de Tenerife; the other week-days, from Los Cristianos. With Hierro, via La Gomera, Monday from Santa Cruz de Tenerife and Wednesday and Friday from Los Cristianos.
Service with the Peninsula is maintained by the Transmediterranean Company with several weekly sailings. Information: Marina, 3. Tel. 24 78 75.
In addition, international transatlantic steamers arrive at Santa Cruz de Tenerife carrying travellers to and from Europe, America, South America and Africa.

URBAN AND INTERURBAN BUS SERVICE

Santa Cruz de Tenerife and its outskirts are linked by 15 buslines. There are also several lines that link the capital with towns in the interior. The buses are called guaguas. Blue buses run within the city limits; red buses, out of town. Out-of-town buses depart from Avda. Tres de Mayo s/n. Information: Titsa. Tel. 21 81 22.
Apart from these regular services, different travel agencies organize others to the tourist resorts on the island.

TEIDE AERIAL CABLE CAR: TECHNICAL CHARACTERISTICS

Length of journey, 2.482 m. (8,143 ft.).
Difference of altitude, 1,199 m. (3934 ft.).
Departure from an altitude of 2,356 m. (7,730 ft.).
Arrival at an altitude of 3,555 m. (11,633 ft.).
Maximum speed, 8 m. (26 ft.) per second.
Engine power, 1,200 HP.
Cabin capacity, 35 persons.
Duration of journey, 8 minutes.

CAR RENTALS

SANTA CRUZ DE TENERIFE

DELSU, S.L. General Franco, 116.
GARAGE ATLANTICO. Rambla General Franci, 20.
AUTOS LASALLE, La Salle, 38.
AUTOS SIMAGO. La Rosa, 93.
AUTOS NUMANCIA. Numancia, 21.
AUTOS TANAUSU. Méndez Núñez.
AUTOS SPORT. Dr. Guigou, 32.
AVIS. Airport.
HERTZ. Airport.

PUERTO DE LA CRUZ

AUTOS TENERIFE. Zamora, 11.
AUTOS TENERIFE. Valois, 13.
AUTOS TENERIFE. Puerto Viejo, 23.
ALTOUR. Santo Domingo, 22.
DELSU. Valois, 44.
ANAGA. Hotel Las Vegas.
MONTECARLO. Zamora, 23.
AVIS. Avda. Venezuela, 13.
AUTOS ROMAR. Calvo Sotelo, 12.
AUTOS FAVORIT, Gasolinera Belair.
HERTZ. Santo Domingo, 24.
AUTOS MONTES. Calvo Sotelo, 59.
AUTOS MARTIANEZ. Calvo Sotelo, 48.

FILLING STATIONS

SANTA CRUZ DE TENERIFE

DISA. Avda. 3 de Mayo.
DISA. Avda. Anaga, s/n.
SHELL. Avda. 3 de Mayo, s/n.
SHELL. El Ramonal, Carretera de la Laguna.
CRUZ DEL SEÑOR. General Mola, s/n.
TEXACO. Carretera de San Andrés.
GARAJE VANDEWALLE. Santa Rosalía, 63.

PUERTO DE LA CRUZ

DISA. Valois, s/n.
SHELL. Las Arenas.
TEXACO. Carretera del Botánico.

TRAVEL AGENCIES

SANTA CRUZ DE TENERIFE

VIAJES ATLANTIDA. San José, 20. Te 24 59 79.
VIAJES BLANDY. La Marina, 27. Te 28 13 00.
VIAJES CLUB DE VACACIONES. Jiméne Díaz, 1. Tel. 22 76 30.
VIAJES FERNANDO POO. La Marina, 1 Tel. 24 20 77.
VIAJES MARSANS. San José, 1. Te 24 64 06.
VIAJES ECUADOR, S.A. Pilar, 6. Te 24 60 75.
VIAJES MELIA. Pilar, 9. Tel. 24 41 50.
VIAJES SOLYMAR. Villalba Hervás, 15. Te 24 70 82.
VIAJES MONTEMAR, S.A. Avda. Anaga, 1! T. 28 49 00.
VIAJES WAGONS LITS COOK. Pilar, 2. Te 24 66 83.

PUERTO DE LA CRUZ

VIAJES MELIA. Avda. Generalísimo, 2 Tel. 38 00 62.
VIAJES INSULAR, S.A. Avda. Generalísim 15. T. 38 02 62.
VIAJES ALIADOS. Avda. Generalísimo, s Tel. 37 25 75.
VIAJES ATLANTIDA. Sargentos Provision les, s/n. T. 38 14 24.
VIAJES BLANDY. Avda. Generalísim núm. 10. Tel. 37 28 19.
VIAJES CEVASA. Avda. Generalísim núm. 10. Tel. 37 31 81.
VIAJES CLUMBA. Carretera Botánico. Te 38 27 50.
VIAJES CYRASA. Santo Domingo, s/n. Te 37 24 99.
VIAJES ECUADOR. Avda. Generalísim s/n. Tel. 37 21 63.
VIAJES BARCELO. Avda. Generalísimo, 2 T. 38 22 50.
VIAJES CANARIAS EXPRESS, S.L. Aveni Generalísimo, s/n. T. 38 11 24.
VIAJES CLUB DE VACACIONES. José Ant nio, 4. T. 38 25 50.
VIAJES CORONA, S.A. Calvo Sotelo, 43. 38 25 70.

IAJES MARSANS. Avda. Generalísimo, s/n. Tel. 37 15 79.

IAJES PAUKNER. Avda. Generalísimo, s/n. Tel. 37 00 40.

IAJES KUONI. Calvo Sotelo, 66. Teléfono 38 08 00.

'IAJES SOLYMAR. Avda. Gral. Franco, s/n. Tel. 37 24 40.

'IAJES TURIST CANARIAS. Playa de Martianez, s/n. Tel. 37 14 88.

'IAJES LIDER, S.A. Calvo Sotelo, 58. Tel. 38 21 00.

'IAJES MACARI. Avda. Generalísimo, 1. Tel. 38 01 16.

AIR LINES

ANTA CRUZ DE TENERIFE

3ERIA. Avda. Anaga, 23. T. 28 80 00.

IR FRANCE. San José, 6. T. 24 75 90.

C.L.M. San José, 25. Tel. 24 45 47.

UFTHANSA. Villalba Hervás, 19. Tel. 24 44 35.

SAS. Avda. Anaga, 43. T. 27 17 00.

WISSAIR. Avda. Anaga, 37. T. 27 64 99.

3RITISH CALEDONIAN. Betancour Alfonso, 6. T. 24 48 75.

'ANAM. Dr. J. Naveiras, s/n. Tel. 28 54 60.

UERTO DE LA CRUZ

3ERIA. Avda. de Colón, s/n. Tel. 37 16 00.

UFTHANSA, Avda. Generalísimo, s/n. Tel. 37 19 60.

UA. Avda. Venezuela, 6. Tel. 37 27 49.

STEAMSHIP LINES AND SHIPPING AGENTS

ANTA CRUZ DE TENERIFE

HLERS RAHN, S.A. Villalba Hervás, núm. 2. Tel. 24 14 90.

UCONA. La Marina, 3. Tel. 24 78 75.

EPSA. Avda. 3 de Mayo. Tel. 28 14 00.

CIA. TRANSATLANTICA ESPAÑOLA. Pilar, 38. Tel. 28 71 61.

CONSIGNACIONES NAVIERAS INTERNACIONALES. Dr. G. Coviella, 5. Tel. 27 98 51.

CONSIGNATARIA INSULAR, S.L. Avenida Anaga, 19. Tel. 28 73 00.

CONSVASCA, S.L. San Francisco, 67. Tel. 28 06 60.

CORPORACION IBERO AFRICANA. San Francisco, 9. Tel. 24 30 66.

CORY HERMANOS. La Marina, 27. Tel. 28 91 00.

ANTONIO CRUZ GONZALEZ. La Marina, 3. Tel. 24 35 00.

E.C.O.P.E.S.A. Bethencourt Alfonso, 4. Tel. 24 77 67.

ELDER DEMPSTER (Canary Islands). Avenida Anaga, s/n. Tel. 27 64 00.

FRUCASA. Avda. Anaga, s/n. Tel. 24 52 65.

GUILLERMO OLSEN Y CIA. Avda. Anaga, 31. Tel. 27 17 00.

HAMILTON y CIA. Avda. Anaga, 39. Tel. 27 32 00.

HERRERA HERNANDEZ. San Antonio, 1. Tel. 24 37 74.

BERGE Y CIA. La Marina, 15. Tel. 24 72 75.

IMPROCO, S. A. E. Calzadilla, 38. Tel. 28 01 00.

LEDESMA Y CIA, S.L. La Marina, 15. Tel. 28 97 00.

MARITIMA MIDWAY, S.A. la Marina, 27. Tel. 28 91 00.

MARITIMA DE TENERIFE. Rambla Pulido, 35. Tel. 22 07 91.

MARITIMA VASCO CANARIA. Villalba Hervás, 3. Tel. 27 25 04.

LUIS MARTIN PEREZ. Castillo, 3. Tel. 24 14 21.

CAMILO MARTINON NAVARRO. La Marina, 3. Tel. 24 57 18.

MILLER Y CIA. La Marina, 27. Tel. 28 91 00.

VDA. E HIJOS DE MOLOWNY, S.A. La Marina, 21. Tel. 24 44 59.

NAVICASA. Avda. Anaga, 23. Tel. 28 71 16.

TRANSAMERICA, S.A. José Murphy, 4. Tel. 24 76 07.

IGNACIO RIVERO MESA. Rambla General Franco, 159. Tel. 27 23 96.

ALVARO RODRIGUEZ LOPEZ. Av. Anaga, 37. Tel. 27 51 00.

VAPORES SUARDIAZ, S.A. Avda. 3 de Mayo, 4. Tel. 24 22 95.

THEATERS AND CINEMAS

SANTA CRUZ DE TENERIFE

TEATRO GUIMERA. Plaza de la Isla de Madera.

TEATRO BAUDET. General Mola, 10.

TEATRO SAN MARTIN. San Martín.

CINE REX. Méndez Núñez, 3.

CINE VICTOR. Plaza de la Paz.

ROYAL VICTORIA. La Rosa.

CINEMA VICTORIA. General Mola.

CINE PRICE. Salamanca, 10.

CINE LA PAZ. Plaza de la Paz.

CINE NUMANCIA. Numancia, 18.

CINE GRECO. Velázquez.

REAL CINEMA. La Rosa, 44.

CINE TENERIFE. General Mola, s/n.

CINE PRINCESA. Princesa Dacil, 31.

CINE DELTA. Barrio de la Salud.

CINE MODERNO. San Sebastián.

CINE PLAZA. Plaza de Toros (Open in Summer).

CINE BUENOS AIRES. La Costa, s/n.

CINE COSTASUR. Barriada Garcia Escámez.

CINE FRAGA. Crra. Rosario, km. 4,8.

PUERTO DE LA CRUZ

CINE CHIMISAY. José Antonio, 11.

CINE OLIMPIA. Pza. Genera, Franco, 13.

CINE VERA. Carretera general.

DISCOTHEQUES AND NIGHT CLUBS

SANTA CRUZ DE TENERIFE

CHAYOFA. San Pedro Alcántara.

COPACABANA. Avda. a. Romero, 2.

LA CARACOLA. C. de Tabares, 14.

CINTRA CLIB. San José, 20.

SAGA CLUB. Rambla Pulido, 67.

KINGS CLUB. Rambla Gral. Franco, 76.

PUERTO DE LA CRUZ

LOS CAPRICHOS. Avda. Colón, 2.

ALI BABA. Nieves Ravelo.

BALI. Bajos Edificio Avenida.

CABALLO BLANCO. San Telmo, H.S Telmo».

GI-GI. San Telmo, 1.

CINTRA CLUB. Calvo Sotelo, 10.

MAXIM. Avda. del Generalísimo Franco s/n.

COLUMBUS. Playa Martianez.

RENDEZ VOUS. Calvo Sotelo, 17.

TABU. Zamora, 15.

TUSET STREET. Avda. del Generalísimo Franco.

ATLANTIS. Hotel Atlantis.

BULL RING

On the Rambla General Franco you will find the Bull Ring, with a capacity of 7,000. Bullfights are held several times a year.

NATIONALLY SUPPORTED RESORTS IN THE PROVINCE OF SANTA CRUZ DE TENERIFE

ACANTILADO DE LOS GIGANTES. Santiago del Teide.

PLAYA DE LAS TERESITAS. Santa Cruz de Tenerife.

PLAYA DE LAS GAVIOTAS. Santa Cruz de Tenerife.

ALLAO SALVAJE. Adeje.
. GUINCHO. San Miguel.
ALM-MAR (pending). Arona.
N-BEL (pending). Arona.
AYA DE LAS AMERICAS (pending).
Arona-Adeje.

TOURIST DEVELOPMENTS
OF APARTMENTS AND VILLAS

RBANIZACION ROMANTICA I y II. Los
Realejos.
ESA DEL MAR. Tacoronte.
RBANIZACION LA PAZ. Puerto de la Cruz.
RBANIZACION LOS ANGELES. El Sauzal.
ABAIBA. El Rosario.
OSTA CARICIA. El Rosario.
ADA AZUL. El Rosario.
UAJARA. La Laguna.
HAYOFA. Arona.
ANTA MARTA. Arona.
ANTA ANA. Arona
RBANIZACION SAN EUGENIO. Adeje.

BEACHES AND NATURAL
SWIMMING-POOLS

enerife has many picturesque beaches,
mainly with black sand because of its volcanic origin, especially in the North. There
are some with fine, golden sand in the
South of the island. They all have beautiful weather all year long.

e most important are the following: Las
Teresitas, with fine, golden sand brought
from Africa, and Las Gaviotas, in Santa
Cruz; El Arenal, between Bajamar and
Punta del Hidalgo; El Boyuyo, in La Oro-
tava; Martianez, in Puerto de la Cruz;
Playa del Castro in Los Realejos and Playa
de San Marcos, big, with good sand, in
Icod de los Vinos.

Apart from these beaches there is a series of
natural salt-water swimming-pools;
among them are to be mentioned the one
in Bajamar and Punta del Hidalgo, the San
Telmo and Costa Martianez pools in
Puerto de la Cruz, and El Caletón in Garachico.

In the South the most important beaches
are Las Caletillas, El Pozo and La Viuda in
Candelaria; el Puertito in Güimar; Los Roques in Fasnia; Poris de Abona in Arico; in
Granadilla, the famous Medano beach
and La Tejita, both with fine, golden sand;
in San Miguel, Los Abrigos and in Arona,
Las Galletas and Los Cristianos, famous
for its quiet waters and golden sand. In
the Playa de las Américas there are more
beaches, notably Troya. Finally, we mention the beach of La Arena, in Puerto de
Santiago, near Los Gigantes.

In La Palma the beach at Puerto Naos and
that of Los Cancajos, both of fine black
sand, are the most visited.

In Gomera are to be mentioned Vallehermoso, Valle Gran Rey with beautiful
golden sand and Playa Santiago, very picturesque places.

Finally in Hierro, the big natural
swimming-pool El Tamaduste, with calm,
clean water.

I.S.B.N. 84-400-0902-X
Depósito legal: B-7.065-85
RESERVADOS TODOS LOS DERECHOS
PROHIBIDA LA REPRODUCCION
SIRVEN GRAFIC Gran Via 754 - Barcelona

Pta. del Mudo Garafia   Pta Gaviota
                    Barlovento   Espíndola
                    Los Sauces   San Andrés
                    Los Tilos
El Roque   2.351
                                    Puntallana
Punta Gorda   Pico de la Cruz

Tijarate   SANTA CRUZ
                        DE LA PALMA   Parador de
                        Breña alta   LA PALMA   P
     Los Llanos
Tazacorte   El Paso   Breña Baja

Saliente de   Corcovado
las Hoyas   Mazo

Puerto de Naos
                        Cueva de
                        Belmaco
           Tiguérorte

     Las Indias   Las Caletas
        Fuencaliente

Pta. de Fuencaliente

LA PALMA

                              Pta. del Guanche
                    Mocanal   Tamaduste
Pta. del Salmor   VALVERDE
              Guarazoca   P
              Parador Nacional
Pta. de la Dehesa   San Andrés   Pto. de la Estaca
                    Frontera
          Los Llanillos
Sabinosa   Isóra
              1.501
             Malpaso
Pta. Tegena   Taibique   Cabo Bonanza
Playa de los Mozos   Las Playas

Playa Calcosas   Cueva del Gaterón

                    Pta. Restinga

HIERRO